#Know
the
Truth

#Know the Truth

Why Knowing Who You Are
Changes Everything

GORDANA BIERNAT

HAY HOUSE

Carlsbad, California • New York City
London • Sydney • New Delhi

Contents

Acknowledgements   ix

Introduction   xiii

How to use this book   xvii

Sharing my truths   xviii

Synchronicity   xxii

**Part 1: Why Knowing Who You Are
Changes Everything**

Who am I? Why am I here?   3

Your point of power   6

'Secret' knowledge   8

Thinking and knowing   10

Everything is consciousness   12

Frequency and YOU   16

Desire and YOU   21

Reality, manifestation and YOU   27

You are perfect as you are   31

**Part 2: Why Understanding Your Place in
Time and Space Changes Everything**

Oneness   35

There is only YOU   38

The veil of forgetfulness 39

'In here' and 'out there' 42

YOU matter! 45

The dilemma of describing ONE 46

The flow of eternal time 47

Part 3: Why Understanding the Nature of Your Thoughts Changes Everything

Thoughts matter 51

Beliefs 52

The pliant nature of your beliefs 54

Ego 58

Stay creative and open 61

Negativity and struggle 63

Worry and daydreaming 68

Part 4: Why Finding Your Flow Changes Everything

Change is the only constant 75

Change is your natural state of being 79

Do what YOU love 82

'Right' knowledge 85

Birthrights, freedoms and needs 86

Part 5: Why Understanding the Nature of Fear Changes Everything

What is fear? 89

YOU are real. Fear is not 92

Contents

Change fear of rejection into power 96

Fear is a liar 99

Negativity and Source 100

Come closer 105

**Part 6: Why Imagination Is Your Tool
of Creation**

Source of creativity 109

YOU are creative 112

Creativity equals courage 114

Part 7: Why Now Is Your Point of Power

NOW and the illusion of time 119

Memories 123

Change your past 126

Set your intention 130

I am 133

Part 8: Why God = You

What is GOD? 137

Who are YOU? 138

Dying Gods and Goddesses 139

Why knowing who YOU are matters 140

YOU in relation to others 141

Part 9: Why You = Love

YOU are LOVE   145

YOU are the shining ONE   149

Perfect imperfections   153

YOU are your biggest asset   155

Part 10: Why You Are the Point of Creative Manifestation

YOU are the Imaginer   161

Obstacles   170

Thought seeds   173

Part 11: Why You Are Responsible for Your Reality

Heaven or hell? Your choice   179

YOU and your 'demons'   182

Your world and the 'real world'   186

Worker or Creator? Your choice   191

Your 'Buddha-In-Disguise'   195

The Wisdom Keeper   200

The creative side of responsibility   203

About the Author   211

Acknowledgements

1 | *Children see magic*
where grown-ups seek logic.

To my son, Hubert:

Your ability to share unconditional love with all sentient beings inspires me to higher thought and puts me in direct communication with the pureness of my soul. Just being around you reconnects me to *who* I truly am. Mothering you, I found my true self. Thank you for allowing me into your beautiful world.

2 | *When I look into your eyes*
I find my most beautiful self.
YOU and I are ONE.

To my husband, Gregor:

Your relaxed attitude to life and your focus on the joyous aspects of being, remind me of *why* my soul has taken root in this physical reality. You inspire me to allow the pleasures of being alive in this space and time to come forth through me. When my 'compass' is astray, I look for you. YOU are my North Star. Around you, everything is possible. Thank you for co-creating this reality with me.

3 | *Every ONE of us*
      | *is a story in progress.*

To Sheri Salata:

My eternal gratitude to you for believing in me – and for inspiring me to dream even bigger and grow beyond my comfort zone. You are a source of joy and power combined.

4 | *Knowing who you are*
      | *changes the world.*

To Oprah Winfrey:

Thank you for recognizing the SuperSoul teacher in me and for including me in your incredible SuperSoul100 team. Together, we raise world consciousness.

5 | *When we choose to see*
      | *the best in others,*
      | *we remind them of*
      | *who they truly are.*

To my Hay House tribe:

Thank you Michelle Pilley, Amy Kiberd, Tom Cole, Julie Oughton, Diane Hill, Jo Burgess and Debra Wolter for seeing the best in me and for co-creating a place in time and space for my book to manifest. You showed me how dreaming big always pays off.

6 | *You are the brave ONE*
holding the key
to open your heart
and set yourself free.

Thank you dear reader and truth seeker for allowing my thoughts into your reality. If, by synchronistic luck, I should happen to spot you sitting and reading my book, allow me to sit down beside you. I would love to hear your thoughts.

Introduction

This book came to life in a somewhat unusual way. Even though I had been 'storing' it in my heart for as long as I can remember, the words and sentences were not always clear to me. When I closed my eyes, I could flip the book's pages in my mind and almost read the titles of the chapters. Sometimes, I could even feel the touch of its cover and sense its weight in my hand.

But no matter how hard I tried, I could not see the actual words in it. Writing a book felt like opening the gates to my inner self, allowing the outer world to enter. The vulnerability imbedded in that thought and the fear of feeling 'wide open', kept blurring the words and sentences, denying me the joy of sharing my thoughts in the complete form of a book.

One day, my husband showed me a piece of paper on which was a passage of text. I recognized it as my own words, but I could not remember when I had written them. The reason the words were unfamiliar was because he had assembled eight of my tweets and put them together, one after the other, creating half a page of text. (Tweets are short messages sent on Twitter, a news and social networking website – twitter.com. My Twitter handle [username] is @Mypowertalk.)

The odd thing was, even though I had written and posted the tweets independently of each other – days or even weeks apart – they integrated brilliantly and made perfect sense. It was as if I had written the whole passage in one breath.

It dawned on me that the reason I could not 'see' the words in the book of my mind was because I was looking for them in the 'wrong' place. They were right there... in front of me. I realized that my book, #KnowTheTruth, was already written, by me – only in 'chunks' of 140 characters at a time on Twitter.

When the fear of being vulnerable became stronger than the joy of sharing my important messages, the Universe jumped in, and as usual in my life, did its 'thing'. Looking at the words on the piece of paper my husband gave me, I grasped the beauty of the synchronistic force behind the doings of the Universe. Sometimes when we don't do what we came here to do, the Universe does it *for* us by silently working *through* us.

What this book is about

#KnowTheTruth is an inspirational book based on my straightforward and empowering tweets about who we are and why we are here.

When I first started sharing my insights on Twitter, I was amazed at how they resonated with people of all cultures, religions, ages and gender. And today, when I have more than 300,000 followers on Twitter, I love that it has connected me to people who are on the same path as I am – we are raising consciousness by seeking our own truth.

Readers from all over the world write to me, sharing their stories about how my guidance is assisting them on a daily basis, and how they use my messages on Twitter to make important decisions easier, calm down before a speech, prepare for a meeting or just align with their true self. By asking, 'What do I need to focus on now?' or 'What is my message for today?' or 'What's Gordana up to?' they allow the synchronicity of my Twitter feed to guide and help them.

This book is an extension of that, and it is designed to do the same for you. Within its short chapters you will find numbered 'truth thoughts' that are based on my original tweets. Each numbered truth thought is a statement reconnecting you to universal truths about who we are, why we are here and the importance of remembering our true self. The truth thoughts are accompanied by exploratory text that goes deeper – amplifying, explaining and extending their meaning.

The information imbedded within – and in-between – the truth thoughts will give you a feeling of ease because it 'makes sense' in a somewhat senseless and spiritually 'disconnected' world. In this age of endless information, streaming from all directions, most of us are looking for instant connection with something that intuitively feels like the truth.

One glance – that is all we are prepared to give it. It is as if we intuitively know that all it actually takes is a few short seconds to reconnect to our own inner truth. Why is this so? Because the truth is never complicated or irrational; the truth always feels easy and right.

7 | *Put your hand*
on your HEART.
Feel it beat.

It is a God-given GIFT.
Listen to it.

It will always
tell you the TRUTH.

The truth has the ability to change our inner emotional frequency and as a result, alter our outer reality. Without demanding any effort in return. All we have to do is allow it into our reality as a thought, belief or action.

#KnowTheTruth will help you reconnect to who you truly are – to the essence of your being, to your innermost truth. It will not talk to your conditioned beliefs, but to the human being in you. And it will do so in a quick, clear-cut way, helping you remember your inherent greatness and immediately improving the quality of your everyday life.

I want to convey my message in the most unconcealed, concise and direct way possible, without making it too simple or too basic. The clarity and certainty of every 'truth thought' will offer you the benefit of 'no doubt', which often tends to speed up the process of reconnecting to the powerful source that we all are.

How to use this book

#KnowTheTruth can be read from cover to cover, or you can use it as a tool – a personal oracle if you like – to evoke synchronicity at *your* command. If you have an unresolved issue or need guidance from your Higher Self, just ask: 'What do I need to know right now? What is my message?'

Then, think of a number between 1 and 231, and look up the 'truth thought' attached to your chosen number. Since the number you pick will be random, the truth thought will become a 'meaningful coincidence' synchronistically connected to you and reflecting your current mood of heart.

All the truth thoughts in the book have ONE purpose – to help you heighten your perception of your self by reminding you of who you truly are, what you need to know in this particular moment and how to act in the situation or obstacle ahead.

Your thoughts determine your future experiences. To change your future, you must first change your current mood, thoughts and emotions. The world 'outside' is a mirror of your mind. Use that mirror to alter your future 'image'.

Sharing my truths

8 | *It is not what you say out loud,*
but what you THINK when you are alone
that has the greatest impact
on how your life unfolds.

Even though I see myself as a socially interactive being, I was a very lonely child. Somehow, my thoughts about *my* world kept disconnecting me from the 'real' world 'outside'. The more I tried to adapt myself to the 'real' world, the further away from the real *me* I seemed to be.

My attempts to adjust who I was, in order to 'fit in' and belong, felt strange and awkward, and I often chose to escape the 'real' world by drifting into my 'safe' world within. I have always had a spiritual way of looking at existence, but during my childhood all the thoughts and wonderings went on in complete silence, inside my head. There, I felt I could be myself. No misunderstandings. No judging. No fear.

The reason I always preferred my own company – and constantly chose my lonely and silent inner world – cannot be explained in simple psychological terms and platitudes, often used by the grown-ups in my childhood when trying to describe my behaviour – such as: 'She is an introvert' or 'She is just a shy child.' I think that to really understand our past, we must view it from a higher and more expanded perspective.

The way I see it, my spiritual self chose, for a good reason, to be born as a girl in an intellectually and emotionally harsh environment in which children and women had little or no right to speak up. With an emotionally disconnected yet very dominant father, and an extremely submissive mother, my childhood was a place where insanity and anxiety walked hand in hand, creating a reality filled with worry and emotional distress.

Instead of seeking happiness and joy in my life, avoiding fear became my way of interacting with my outer reality. There is a big difference between these two paths through life. Seeking happiness is all about trusting yourself and always following your excitement, no matter what. Avoiding fear is exactly the opposite: it is shutting your self down and ignoring your own truths and beliefs in favour of someone else's, just to be loved and accepted.

As a child, I was not capable of sensing the difference between the two paths. And more importantly, I did not see the choice. I simply reacted to my distressing outer reality by avoiding it and by seeking my own truth, joy and calmness within.

This, I have come to understand later in life, is the good reason my Higher Self chose the 'lousy' settings of my childhood. Being born into a dysfunctional family not only gave me an opportunity, it literally pushed me to quietly explore my truth within. So, at a very early age, I knew that the only one I could speak to about my thoughts or about reality and the fabric of the Universe was my self. This basically meant the 'conversation' always contained three 'participants': ME (my physical mind), MYSELF (my spirit and soul) and I (All That Is).

'All That Is' can be replaced with anything that fits your beliefs. To me, 'All That Is' and 'God' are interchangeable concepts', but I prefer to use the term 'All That Is' because I find it less polysemous and not as charged with inherent meaning as the word 'God'. What I am talking about here is infinite consciousness permeating and containing everything that *was*, *is* and will ever *be*. A religious believer would call it God. A spiritual person would refer to it as Source. A scientist would define it as the quantum field containing everything in a state of constant probability. Some would label it the Universe.

I like to call it All That Is. The way I see it, all these 'labels' are only different names for one and the same thing – infinite consciousness unconditionally accepting and sustaining our existence.

It is amazing how loneliness can urge you to ask questions but then force you to patiently wait for the quiet answers from within. At bedtime I would spend hours imagining things and exploring my inner reality. One night while lying in bed, I closed my eyes and tried really hard to imagine 'the last star' at the outpost of the Universe. Even though I 'roamed' the Universe back and forth in my mind, I could not 'figure out' an ending edge. All I could see was sparkling stars.

Every time I thought I had reached 'the edge', a funny sensation arose in the back of my head and the Universe of my mind expanded, giving birth to millions of new stars and galaxies. My imagination is infinite, I reasoned, so maybe the 'real' night sky could give me a better clue. Surely the 'real' world would be more precise?

I got up and looked through my bedroom window at the dark sky, filled with sparkling stars. And that is when it hit me. I closed my eyes – stars. I opened them again – stars. I realized that there is no difference between the thoughts 'inside' my head and the reality 'outside' it. No matter what I did, the sky stayed dark and the stars kept sparkling. And no matter how far I looked, I could not find 'the edge'.

At the age of 11, I became aware that, in essence, 'inside' and 'outside' are the same. I could 'see' the stars and the Universe, even with my eyes closed, because my thoughts and the fabric of the Universe are made of the same 'stuff'.

What I experienced is a universal esoteric truth that changed me and the way I perceive myself. It was a profound moment for me, filling my body with the tingling 'aha' feeling of a truth at the point of no return.

I took my first *conscious* step within and started, from that vantage point, a lifelong adventure exploring the boundaries of what seems to be 'the without'. At the time, it was my secret view of reality because I could not share it with anyone. Now, I am choosing to expand my truths and the boundaries of my Universe, by sharing it with you.

Synchronicity

9 | *Everything is interconnected,*
infinitely changing and manifesting
through perfect synchronicity.

For a while now, synchronicity has been playing an increasing role in my reality. It started calling my attention with mere 'coincidences' and 'what-are-the-odds' situations. Then it got more 'daring', showing off in the most incredible settings. For instance, I would sit down, open a book and with a deep relaxing sigh I would start reading. The first words I would see were: 'With a deep sigh...'.

Most people would say that an event like that is just a meaningless coincidence. But to me, it is the Universe speaking through the language of synchronicity, showing me the entanglement of my inner psychic realm and the external physical world. It is also giving me a glimpse of the magic behind the scenes – the way everything is interconnected beyond the notion of time and space.

The Universe does not just 'hear' what I say. It seems to *know* what I feel and truly believe. Through the synchronicity of such an event the Universe is showing me that what I 'ask' for, it immediately and unconditionally answers. Beyond the smallest 'bits' of physical matter on the invisible level of reality, *I* am interacting in perfect synchronicity with a *conscious* Universe. Which, from my earthly point of view, makes the Universe my partner in creation.

10 | *Coincidence is just a disguise for something much more profound and magnificent.*

We experience synchronicity when our mind is open and our awareness is heightened. It often turns up in our daily life as 'meaningful coincidences' or a 'stroke of luck'. When we are open to it, synchronicity 'pops up' as signs that reveal the interconnectedness of our world and the boundlessness of inner and outer reality.

> *'Synchronicity is the coming together of inner and outer events in a way that cannot be explained by cause and effect, and that is meaningful to the observer.'*
>
> CARL GUSTAV JUNG

Usually, synchronicity appears at random and seems to be at play when our inner thoughts and outer situations coincide in time – connecting against all odds in an apparently meaningful way.

The peculiar thing about synchronicity is that it carries information that is meaningful to the observer, yet it cannot be explained in a rational way by a normal sequence of cause and effect. In other words, it connects you with the Universe on a very deep, personal level.

I will let a passage from *The Kybalion*, a book about the seven principles of reality written by three unnamed authors and first published in 1908, highlight the 'invisible' structure of chance and the connectedness underlying chance and coincidence:

> *'Every cause has its effect; every effect has its*
> *cause; everything happens according to Law;*
> *chance is but a name for Law not recognized.'*
>
> THE KYBALION

Albert Einstein called this strange connectedness 'spooky action at a distance', while quantum physicists use the term 'quantum entanglement' to describe the infinite bond between the smallest bits of physical reality.

The more we allow synchronicity into our lives, the more meaning we find in random events, words, signs and situations. And the easier it becomes to 'talk' to the Universe, because synchronicity seems to be the underlying pattern – or, as it is expressed in *The Kybalion*, the 'Law not recognized' yet – in the fabric of the Universe.

11 | *Viewed from a higher perspective,*
you are always at the right time
and at the right place to experience
what you need right NOW.

The way I see it

Part 1

Why Knowing Who You Are Changes Everything

Who am I? Why am I here?

12 | *I am an incredible,*
deliberate creator.

On the surface, it might seem like a simple question: 'Who am I?'

'I am Gordana Biernat, and I am a writer.'

However, describing who I am to its fullest extent, and in an all-encompassing way, becomes much trickier. If I try to define *all* of me, in one sentence, I lose the words. I simply cannot describe myself as any *one* thing or quality, because that would be like focusing on bits and fractions of who I truly am. Or like looking at a puzzle with missing pieces – annoyingly denying me the whole picture. It could never truthfully describe my whole being.

The difficulty in answering the question 'Who am I?' lies in trying to dress in words something that is not only *beyond* words, but beyond time and space itself. How do you describe the ONE *thinking, choosing* and *perceiving* in YOU?

If I wrote you a poem, you could *feel* who I am. If I painted a picture, you could *see* who I am. But describing myself in such terms as 'I am an art historian' or 'I am a mentor', would not give you the entire truth about who I am. It would only present to you a chosen 'mask', 'part' or 'facet' of the whole 'picture'.

So, what *is* the whole picture?

Exploring who I am presents a paradox to me because the more I *know* who I truly am, the harder it gets to *describe* who I am. The closest I can come to a truthful answer is: 'I am All That Is – pure consciousness – experiencing itself through the *passions* and *desires* of Gordana Biernat. My personality is focused in my body. My body is in my consciousness and my consciousness is infinite, eternal and everywhere.' It is mind-boggling.

And what of the second question: 'Why am I here?' For a long time I thought that my mission here on Earth was to *find* my spiritual source – where the essence of my being and soul springs to life from the infinite consciousness of All That Is – and *become one* with it. As time has passed I have come to realize that I am, have always been, and will eternally remain, my own source.

Nothing needs to be *found*. I do not need to *become* anything. *I already am.* All I have to do is find *my way* of *expressing* what *I am.*

I think that what I am actually doing here on Earth is having the privilege of exploring physical reality. This means enjoying the sky, the sun, food, the rain... It means interacting with other beings, loving, crying, thinking, laughing... Simply being.

I am here to explore the physicality of this reality in all its perfect imperfection. I will know my source when I return to it. Now, my spirit is here to grasp how it feels to be human. This goes for all of us.

13 | *We are not physical beings*
in search of our soul.
We are souls experiencing
a world of matter.
We have all the power
we will ever need, already within.

If I had to narrow the question down to describing my physical being, my earthly self, I would say, 'I am a mother, I am a soulmate and I am a seeker.'

I really, really, really need to explore my truths about the creation of reality.

I have a son, and I want him to live in a world filled with kind, loving, sentient, conscious beings. Because, once we truly understand the simple truth that we are the creators and consumers of our reality, we will start being the incredible, deliberate creators we were born to be. And start creating a world worthy of who we truly are.

Your point of power

14 | *NOW is your point of power.*
It is where YOU are.
NOW is forever.
It is always NOW.

The only place in time and space where YOU are is NOW. The only place in time and space where you can take action is NOW. And NOW, and NOW and NOW... Because you see, it is always NOW. Everything that was, is and will ever be can only be found in the eternal NOW. NOW is actually all there is.

There is no past and no future, unless you think of it. Think about that.

15 | *YOU are the creator*
of your past and future,
and your point of power
is NOW.

| *Enjoy your present.*

16 | *Breathe... in... and... out.*
Allow your consciousness to
expand... and... retract.

NOW is a 'place' where there
is NO-time and NO-space.
It is infinite, eternal, here and nowhere.
It is ALWAYS and it is NOW.

Breathe... in... and... out.
Allow your consciousness to
expand... and... retract.

You are ALWAYS safe NOW.

If you like what your reality is reflecting NOW, stay in the moment and enjoy your being. On the other hand, if you do not like what you are experiencing in your reality NOW, then NOW is your point of power to make a change. Your thoughts NOW create your future presence.

'Secret' knowledge

17 | *When your pursuit of wisdom is sincere and persistent, what you need can NOT be hidden from you.*

The truth is that *all* knowledge is available to *everyone*. Everything you desire to know lies in plain sight. The trick is to ask the 'right' questions and to look in the 'right' places.

There is a difference between 'hidden' *esoteric* (non-conventional) knowledge and 'popular' *exoteric* (conventional) knowledge. Exoteric knowledge is practically thrown at you. It is presented everywhere: stating and confirming beliefs about how society should function and proposing models for how you should behave and act in order to 'fit into' the prevailing norm.

Exoteric knowledge is easy to access; in fact, it is hard not to be affected by it because the government, the media and the education system offer it for 'free' and shower you with 'benefits' when you learn and repeat.

Esoteric knowledge, on the other hand, is perceived as hidden or secret, because *you* must actively seek it in order to find it – meaning it takes a *conscious action* to become aware of it. The funny thing about this 'secret' knowledge is that the 'right' place to look for it is *within* YOU.

Every question you have and every answer you seek is 'hidden' within YOU. Our society would change dramatically if more people realized this truth. Esoteric knowledge is 'secret' because no one but YOU can reveal it. YOU are the source.

18 | *You can never turn your back on truth. It is everywhere, silently waiting for you to find it.*

Thinking and knowing

19 | *An aha moment feels good –*
not because you think something NEW,
but because you REMEMBER
what you already KNOW.

The difference between thinking and knowing is that thinking is a sequential process, while knowing is *being*.

Thinking is an activity in time that literally requires physical space in your brain. It is based on current beliefs and memories and depends on gathering and processing information through the passing of time.

Knowing is momentary understanding. It is a direct connection, beyond physical time and space, between you and All That Is (the quantum field, Source, the Universe, God). Knowing is instant. It takes no time and uses no space. It is an act of being totally in the 'NOW-moment'.

Thinking is a brain activity; knowing is a gut feeling. Thinking is noisy; knowing is quiet. Thinking is movement; knowing is stillness. Thinking is the searching 'light'; knowing is the all-containing 'darkness'. Thinking is yang; knowing is yin. Thinking is connected to matter and the physical aspect of reality; knowing is connected to All That Is and the 'no-time/no-space' invisible aspect of reality. The symbiosis between the two is YOU.

20 | *Thinking is a brain activity.*
Knowing is a gut feeling.
Thinking is movement.
Knowing is stillness.
Thinking takes time.
Knowing is NOW.

Everything is consciousness

21 | *There is consciousness in everything*
and everything is in constant creation.

Can you see the beauty
of your existence?

Consciousness is the underlying structure of everything. It is the energy that runs and maintains the Universe, making the very fabric of it by acting as 'the glue' connecting all things.

This strongest force in the Universe, consciously holding everything in its right place, seems to reside in the smallest bits of 'nothingness' – or what quantum physicists call the 'infinite field of possibilities'. It is where everything that was, is and will ever be exists. This field of consciousness contains all possibilities as potential bundles of energy 'waiting' for a subjective mind to think, feel or believe it into existence.

So, consciousness is everywhere, and yet we cannot see it. It transcends everything, and yet it is not separate from us. Everything is connected and happens as a flow of energy on a quantum level of reality. Every single leaf is consciously connected to the entire forest: just as you are consciously connected to the entire human race. On a quantum level of physical reality, nothing can exist on its own. Everything exists in relationship to something else. Actually, it is the relationships that define its 'existness'.

22

Everything is ONE,
and at the same time,
everyONE is unique.

We are one consciousness experiencing itself through a multitude of 'focus-points' of awareness. I am consciousness focused into being *me*. You are consciousness focused into being *you*. The difference between your reality and mine is the focus-point of awareness. We are only different *perspectives* of the same consciousness. Therefore, you do not *have* a consciousness; instead, consciousness *contains* you and everything in your reality, including me.

Simply put, consciousness is All That Is. It is infinite potentiality saturating everything. Literally. The question then, is how does infinite potential turn into physical reality?

The interesting thing is that physical reality is, in essence, hollow. The deeper we go into matter, the more space we encounter and the harder it gets to describe what 'physical' reality and 'matter' actually are. If everything is consciousness, then how does consciousness *become* matter? And how does *infinite, eternal* 'being' turn into a *specific finite* experience?

Consciousness is the 'bridge' between the infinite field of possibilities and your physical reality. It is the portal through which your immediate reality is continuously created. In other words, consciousness is the 'darkness' containing everything. Your awareness is the focused 'searchlight' extracting things from it into reality. You are exploring how it feels to transform high-frequency energy into low-frequency energy. Simply put: you are turning thoughts into things. We will be talking more about frequencies later in the book.

23 | *You are simultaneously creating and consuming your own reality.*

Consciousness is your entire Being: your thoughts, feelings, intuition and will. Your body and mind are its material vehicles in your physical reality. It is inside and outside you. You are the connection between macrocosm and microcosm, between above and below and between inside and outside.

Your physical reality contains what you focus into being by giving it your subjective attention. External conditions in your reality are just a reflection of your internal beliefs and thoughts. What you believe becomes 'real' in your reality.

24 | *You are the Imaginer, Creator and Explorer of reality. You are All That Is.*

Can you see the beauty of your existence? Do you feel the immense creative power with which you have been endowed?

25 | *You create your own reality. Everything in your reality is your creation.*

Relax. Play.
Be creative.

Allow your consciousness to stretch out. Expand your reality. And mine.

Frequency and YOU

26 | *You attract things of the same frequency as YOU.*

How conscious of what YOU really want, are you?

The creation of your reality is not so much a law of attraction pulling things *to* you, as it is a law of corresponding (equal) frequency – working *through* you via your thoughts, feelings and beliefs.

The law of corresponding frequency works regardless of whether you are deliberately thinking, randomly daydreaming, visualizing, worrying, dreaming, dreading or wishing out loud. It mirrors your beliefs exactly and unconditionally.

When you believe something to be true about yourself or your reality, you are sending information to your source in All That Is (the quantum field, Source, the Universe, God) about how your reality 'seems' to you.

You are sharing data about what you feel are the most probable outcomes in your reality. Your beliefs then align your frequency to the matching frequency in the quantum field and manifest your chosen vibration through you for you to see, feel, hear or taste in your physical reality.

And here is the trick:

27 | *You cannot perceive a frequency other than the one you have tuned in to with your thoughts, emotions and beliefs.*

It is like a radio station. There are other frequencies 'out there' but you can only hear the one to which your 'radio' is tuned. To change your frequency you have to change your thoughts, your feelings and what you believe.

If your beliefs are incongruent with your thoughts, words and actions, they annihilate each other and the status quo is preserved. Nothing new happens – everything stays the same and there is no change. That is why a pep talk will work *only* if you believe what is being said to you.

If both your thoughts and your beliefs are negative, the outcome will be as negative as you imagine it to be. If your thoughts are positive and match your beliefs perfectly, the outcome will be as positive as you imagine it to be. In other words, you receive what you consciously or subconsciously believe.

28 | *Your frequency is the REQUEST.*

Identical vibration in the quantum field is the ANSWER.

Manifestation is the RESULT.

In other words:

29 | *Life does not happen TO you,*
it happens THROUGH you.

Think about this: if everything in the Universe is made of energy vibrating at different frequencies, then our primary sense must in fact be some kind of 'frequency recognition', and not sight, sound, touch, smell and taste. Our five senses are only secondary 'translations' of the initial frequency recognition.

YOU are the one interpreting and directing the sound, taste, look and feel of your Universe. Because what you choose to focus your awareness on – good or bad, joy or sadness, love or hate – becomes the dominant frequency of your reality. We live in a reality that is created through us and has the same frequency as us.

What we believe reality to be, so it is.

30 | *Your frequency is either*
negative (FEAR) or positive (LOVE).
It cannot be both at the same time.
It is your choice.

So in a sense, you are the light in a dark Universe. The darkness of the Universe is not a negative thing. It is the pure consciousness of All That Is densely containing everything. The light of your focused awareness is just a light searching out and extracting things from the infinite darkness of All That Is.

It is your *interpretation* of whatever you shine your awareness on, that gives it meaning. By naming things good, bad, positive, negative, like, don't like, love, hate, beautiful or ugly, YOU give them meaning.

But if you look at it from a broader perspective of reality, what you are encountering and experiencing in different ways is neutral frequencies and vibrations. And *all* the values you attach to the frequencies you choose to explore are *subjective*. *Your* interpretation and perception gives them meaning and content. This is why the Universe needs YOU to exist. YOU give it meaning. Without YOU, there is no meaning. YOU *are* the meaning.

31 | *Everything you 'see' in your reality is there in accordance with your consciousness, your awareness and your frequency.*

There appears to be a misconception that we are only able to create from time to time, or when the spirit moves us. But the law of attraction is a *constant* law, a principle that works *all* the time. That is why it is called a law.

Believing that we create only occasionally or saying that the law of attraction does not work for us, is like suggesting that gravity only works on certain days or in certain locations or only on certain people.

The fact is, you are *always* creating and the law of attraction is *always* working. It is your frequency that determines what you manifest. In other words, you are always sending a frequency with your thoughts, feelings and beliefs, and the Universe is always responding to your specific frequency. The question begging to be asked then, is: 'How do we change frequency?'

32 *Your feelings are indicators of your frequency and your current point of creation.*

To change your future, LOOK for GOOD things NOW.

Have the courage, integrity and grace to say 'no' to negative suggestions from your surroundings. Because:

33 *Mind is a tool with which you create your reality.*

Everything that does not belong in your IDEAL reality, should not be in your THOUGHTS.

Focus on deliberately, actively and intensely finding even the smallest thing to appreciate, feel love for, enjoy, laugh at, be amazed by, be touched by or feel gratitude for. It will instantly change your frequency and align you with your source.

Desire and YOU

34 | *Everything begins as a desire*
to experience something.

Fulfilling your desires is thus
not a luxury, but a purpose in life.

Nature is a magician pulling apples, flowers and butterflies out of its sleeve. *Look what I can do*, it says. *Are you not amused?*

But instead of enjoying the magic of life, we seem to keep asking for its *meaning*. I think I will let Charlie Chaplin, the comedian of all times, put the right perspective on things with his brilliant statement: 'What do you want meaning for? Life is a desire, not a meaning.'

Everything starts out as a desire to experience something. Imagine your source as All That Is (the quantum field, the Universe, God) in total stillness. The moment a desire to experience something sparks into existence, movement is created in the stillness of All That Is and a separation occurs. This prime separation from the source is the beginning of who YOU are. You are God's spark of desire. We all are.

Your source 'desired' you into being because it wants to explore what it is like to experience 'things' for the first time – to know how it feels to see, smell, touch, hear and taste;

how it feels to long for something and how it feels when you free yourself from limitations.

Your source wants to perceive the world through YOU. You are here to experience the physicality of this reality. That is what your spirit desires. It wants to explore the polarities of a physical reality and how it feels to have a choice between light and darkness, 'good' and 'bad'.

This is why the physical reality as we know it seems to contain an equal amount of plus and minus, positive and negative. It is also why, where there is light, there must also be darkness, and why every beginning must have an end. Desires remind us of our mortality and of the evanescence of things, because wanting something awakens immediate awareness of its absence and evokes the fear of losing it.

A desire never leaves us emotionless and balanced; instead, it produces a struggle. Or more precisely, a tension between 'having' and 'not having'. But experiencing the polarity of 'having' and 'not having' can also serve a positive purpose because of its ability to heighten every experience by showing us the contrast.

So, physical existence seems to be closely entangled with desire. Are we embracing or repressing our desires? Are we feeling guilt or joy over our desires? Are we fulfilling or hiding our desires? How we choose to relate to our desires seems to be the whole point of existence.

According to the 17th-century philosopher Thomas Hobbes, 'There is no such thing as perpetual tranquillity of mind while we live here; because life itself is but motion and can never be without desire, nor without fear, no more than without sense.' Without desire, there can be no life. Desire is the prime mover, the initiator of change, the transformer and the fundamental motivator. Actually, it is impossible to exist here without exploring some kind of desire. Even if the desire is to silence your desire, it is still a desire.

You cannot give up desire – it is a part of the game of life and death and of physical reality. You are here to explore how it feels to have a choice between your experiences. Your desires are the purpose in your life because they show you what you are here to experience.

The Upanishads – the four spiritual and philosophical texts that together make up the Vedas, the sacred scriptures of most Hindu traditions – describe the importance and the central meaning desire has in human existence by stating: 'You are what your deepest desire is. As your desire is, so is your intention. As your intention is, so is your will. As your will is, so is your deed. As your deed is, so is your destiny.'

35

*The sum of your desires
is a unique 'fingerprint'
that reveals who you are.*

*Your every desire
is a definer of YOU.*

YOU are your desires.

Your soul is the source of joy and growth. Your physical self is an accumulation of the desires and passions that your soul wishes to explore. The desires and passions are the foundation of your personality and physical identity.

36 | *When you do what you love,*
you are in alignment
with your desires and passions,
which are aligned with
the essence of your source.

Every time you do something you *don't* love, you are out of alignment with your source – out of synchronicity with the frequency of your true self. As a result, you experience sadness, fear, emotional stagnation or physical pain. This is your soul's way of telling you to get back in alignment with your source and put yourself in the vibration of your desires and passions to match its frequency.

Fulfilling your desires is the purpose in your life. It is not some luxurious thing only wealthy people are privileged to do. Going against your own will is as big a 'violation' of it as is doing bad things to others by going against their will.

37 | *Every time you*
deny a desire,
ignore a passion,
neglect a true calling
or silence a truth within you,
your SPIRIT fades.

Follow your BLISS!

Denying yourself your desires, and not exploring them, is to go against your life purpose. When you violate your will by fearing what others might think of you if you express your desires – and as a consequence of that, do not allow the God-given magic of being YOU to manifest – it will give you 'bad karma'. Exactly as if you were to go against another person's will by harming them or forcing them to do something they do not want to.

We live in an unconditionally accepting Universe, which means you are allowed to have any desire you want – as long as you are not harming other sentient beings. When you are exploring your desires, you are closer to your source, and that energy is invigorating, exciting, healing, miraculous, creative and boosting.

Fulfilling your desires heightens your frequency and bypasses time and space because it is directly connected to your timeless, infinite source. That is why time seems to fly when you are absorbed in something you love to do.

Being in your desires alters the chemical processes in your body. Your body reacts to this and invigorates you by giving you more life force that comes directly from your source: from your loving self. It rewards you instantly because you are on the right track, doing the right thing, fulfilling your life purpose.

Used consciously, your desires are an essential part of your 'navigation system' – like an internal GPS – always leading you to the right place in your life.

38 | *YOU are the designer of your PURPOSE.*
YOU are the container of your DESIRES.
YOU are the liberator of your PASSIONS.

Remember that a desire can be so many things – a desire to live, a desire to know, a desire to educate yourself, a desire to stay healthy or a desire to help others. When you choose to follow your heart by doing what you love, you express your uniqueness and that is why YOU are here NOW.

The cool thing is that we all love different things, and that is what makes this world such a wonderful place to be. Nature knows that there is no point or meaning in creation if we all act and think the same way. It is the diversity in what we love that makes creation so exhilarating and exciting.

If you want to make this world a better place, you need to explore who you are and what YOU love. It is important because no one else can give the rest of the world the same thing as you. You are unique. Fulfilling your life purpose by exploring your desires is not a part-time thing or a hobby you do if time permits. It is your life. Own it.

Imagine that everyone on this planet knew what incredible creators we all are. Imagine that everyone knew that we create our reality 24/7 by what we think and do. Imagine what we could create together.

39 | *What you LOVE in your life*
is the MEANING of your life.

Reality, manifestation and YOU

40 | *The ONLY 'thing' you can change is YOU.*
The ONLY 'time' you can change is NOW.
The ONLY 'space' you can change is HERE.

All That Is (the quantum field, Source, the Universe, God) is infinite and eternal. What this actually means is that everything that was, is and will ever be resides within its infinite 'boundaries' and can only be found in the eternal NOW.

There is no *outside*, because everything is *INSIDE*. There is no *when*, because it is eternally *NOW*. There is no *where* or *there*, because it is always HERE. It is All That Is. Nothing more, nothing less. Simply... all... that... is. Infinitely containing everything in the eternal NOW. Everything is HERE and NOW. The 'creation' is already finished.

Every thought already exists in the infinite and eternal All That Is. What YOU are doing when you think, speak, feel and act is manifesting it *through* you by giving it form. You are creating *your* version of it, giving it *your* 'flavour', saturating it with the essence of *your* soul and thus creating a new, unique perspective and a new, unique way of expressing it.

Your frequency determines your experience of what you have attracted and how it will look, feel, taste and sound. Every being on Earth is important because every thought, experience or idea is a unique contribution to the total consciousness experiencing itself through its 'parts'. All That Is manifests itself through YOU and through me and through everyone and everything in this reality.

And since All That Is, is infinite and eternal, then every thought, word, feeling and action stays forever within the boundaries of infinity. Nothing is lost. Everything is saved as an enriching experience, adding value to All That Is.

41 *Every single ONE of us is a unique VIBRATION in a beautiful Symphony of Infinite CREATION.*

YOU are the union between macrocosm and microcosm, between above and below and between inside and outside.

It ALL flows through YOU.

This is why it is so important to know who YOU are and what YOU want to experience and create. Since YOU are the creator of your reality and you create everything in it, whatever you choose to believe to be true – good or bad – will manifest itself through you in your reality: in any shape or form, one way or another.

42 | *You attract whatever you*
focus your mind on –
be it worry or abundance,
fear or joy, love or hate.

It is always your choice.

Whatever you choose to focus your awareness on and create strong beliefs about, will become your immediate reality. This goes for each and every one of us. It does not matter if the beliefs are of a positive vibration (love) or a negative one (fear), the frequency we tune in to through our beliefs, feelings and thoughts will be the one broadcasting our version of reality back to us in the form of a 'solid' reality.

What you believe, you perceive. When you say 'I don't want fear in my life', you tune in to the negative frequency of 'not wanting fear', instead of the positive frequency of 'feeling safe'. You end up 'not wanting' something, instead of 'feeling good'.

We have to become more conscious of the frequency we are tapping in to. Two things that might sound the same can be of a totally different frequency.

Let me give you another example:

43 | *To shift from scarcity to abundance,*
you need to start thinking about what you WANT,
instead of what you do not yet HAVE.

Thinking about what you want is a desire flowing from a positive frequency. Thinking about what you do not yet have is a fear vibrating at a negative frequency. It looks the same, but gives very different results. One taps in to the frequency of abundance, the other to scarcity and lack. Be conscious of your frequency. Focus on the feeling of what you want to experience.

Because:

44 | *The Universe does not just 'hear' what you SAY, it KNOWS what you truly feel and BELIEVE.*

You cannot turn your back on your reality. It is what it is.

45 | *You 'take' your reality with you everywhere.*

You and your reality are ONE.

When YOU change, everything changes.

You are perfect as you are

46 | *You do not become outstanding by working on your weaknesses.*

You become outstanding by focusing entirely on your strengths.

We have been conditioned to believe that if we can just 'fix' our shortcomings and weak spots, we will somehow miraculously become our *best self*. The truth is quite the opposite. By constantly focusing on improving our weaknesses, we become boringly normal and lamely average. Sure, we do fit in... But the question is, fit in to *what*?

When my son was ten, he once said to me as we made our way home from school: 'Mom, I feel like a big circle that the teachers are trying to squeeze into a small box.'

Children have a natural aptitude for expressing their uniqueness – without even thinking about it. They seem to know intuitively that when you are doing what you love, you become more of who you truly are. You expand and you grow. We all want to become our 'best selves', but how can you become outstanding while focusing on your weaknesses – desperately trying to fix yourself and 'fit in' with the crowd?

47 | *You cannot 'fit yourself in' to greatness.*
This can only be done
by embracing and pursuing
your biggest dreams and desires.

To be outstanding, you must dare to stand out. Or more correctly, dare to stand free and acknowledge the fact that you are unlike anyone else. Honour the fact that there is only ONE you. YOU are unique. We all are.

48 | *When you do what you love,*
your best self finds a way
to shine through
in every thought you have
and in every action you take.

You are perfect as you are. Stop fixing yourself. Just figure out what you love to do and concentrate on doing more of that. When you focus entirely on your strengths, the rest magically takes care of itself because where attention goes, energy flows.

And remember, if you feel like a circle, you are simply not meant to live in a box.

49 | *Trying to 'fit in', you become*
one sentence in someone else's story.

Standing out,
YOU are YOUR story.

Part 2

Why Understanding Your Place in Time and Space Changes Everything

Oneness

50 | *All is ONE.*
       ONE is All That Is.
       I am ONE.

As a child I could not get my mind around the concept that I am ONE with everyone else. How could that be possible? Clearly, *I* was separate from the *others*. I was not the same as my mother or my father. I was not the same as my brothers. I was not the same as the children in the schoolyard. I was not the same as anyone on the bus, in our neighbourhood, on the planet, in the Universe... I was me. Just me and no one else.

How could I possibly *be* ONE with everything else when obviously I was the ONE *experiencing* everything else?

How could I be ONE with someone while at the same time experience them as *outside* me and *other* than me? If I am ONE with everything, where do I 'end' and where do you 'begin'? If I am ONE with everything, then what is *outside* me?

I would torment my schoolteacher with these questions – hoping that he, as a grown-up, would have figured it out. It took me years of mind-bending to truly grasp the concept of oneness without losing myself in its synchronistically paradoxical nature.

To come closer to some kind of understanding of the concept of being ONE with everything, I figured I had to start asking the right questions. How would you know who you are or what you are, if you were the only ONE in existence? There would be *nothing* with which to compare yourself. There would be nothing to interact with, to experience, to be passionate about, to love, to explore....

While this scenario would probably be interesting for a while, you would eventually get bored and want something to do or to explore. You would want to interact with something that is *not* you. Something that could surprise you; something that could give you a specific experience.

Let's play with the abstract thought that there is nothing outside of you and that you are the ONE being All That Is. How would you solve the problem of boredom? Since there is nothing outside of you – you are All That Is – there is no option other than to divide yourself into smaller parts of your self, erase the knowledge of your true self in those smaller parts and just for the creative fun of it, give the parts 'roles' to play.

You would then set up a scenario in which the smaller parts would interact with each other and report back to you on their sorrows and joys, fears and love, worries and happy experiences. Every time a part got tired of the role it played, you would give it a different, more interesting scenario to act out.

Since you *know*, *trust* and *love* every part of yourself, you would allow everything to be explored. Nothing would be excluded. Every experience would be unconditionally accepted. In eternity. For the joy of being.

51 | *YOU are the ONE being.*
YOU are the ONE perceiving.
YOU are the ONE experiencing.
YOU are the ONE.

Without YOU, there is no ONE.

Oh, and one more thing... If the Universe is infinite, stretching out in all directions, isn't it safe to assume that no matter where you are, YOU are always in the centre of it? And so am I and so is everything else...Oneness... A funny paradox, isn't it?

There is only YOU

52

You are an infinite soul leaving footprints in the sands of eternal consciousness.

Breathe IN... and OUT ... IN... and OUT.

*The essence of the Universe
is flowing through YOU,
back and forth,
like waves reaching the shore.*

*With every breath you take,
YOU dissolve the 'boundary'
between the Universe and YOU,
and between eternity and NOW.*

*There is no yesterday or tomorrow.
There is only NOW.*

*There is no 'inside' or 'outside'.
There is only YOU.*

The veil of forgetfulness

53 | *Life is about peeking through the veil of forgetfulness.*

What is hidden awakens the joy of revealing it.

Your true self is hidden from you. To make sense of why this is, you must first understand where you come from and what you are doing here.

The way I see it, we are all eternal beings who have chosen to play with time and space and explore the denseness of physical reality. Just for the joy of it.

In order for your Higher Self and *infinite* soul to experience the *finite* physical reality, it needs to focus a part of its consciousness on the 'place' where time and space meet and 'cross.' One could say that X marks 'the spot' in the eternal consciousness of All That Is – where the awareness of being YOU emerges.

By choosing to enter physical life – to incarnate – you become 'crucified' on the 'cross' where time and space intersect. This means that you 'agree' to the rules of 'the game' by confining your self to a physical body, and that you accept the 'limitations' created by the bondage of gravity, time and space.

You are bound to dwell on Earth, to age with the passing of time and to make choices between 'right' and 'wrong'. How materialistic or 'Earthbound' you are, or how fast you age, or what is right and wrong, is up to you to explore, change or free yourself from.

One important limitation that you have to accept when entering physical life, is 'forgetting' your true unlimited, all-knowing and unconditionally loving soul-being. Without this 'veil of forgetfulness', your carnal self (body, mind and soul) would not be able to perceive the duality of light and darkness or love and fear, in the physical world.

Your infinite soul knows that the polarity in the physical world is just an illusion and that everything is ONE NOW. 'Not knowing' is a crucial part of the physical experience, giving you – the human being – the delight of 'finding out'. If you continuously tried to find out everything at once – to lift the veil for good and experience your true self to its fullest – you would see through the illusion and thus lose the pleasure of playing the game.

54 | *The point of being here is to catch glimpses of the magic behind the physical world by being fully present in everything you encounter.*

Everything is yours to play with, to explore, to enjoy – and to learn something new about yourself while you are doing it.

Every time you sense love in someone's heart, feel the calmness of a tree or imagine the world in a raindrop, you 'see' beyond the veil. It is an ongoing process called life, where that which is 'hidden' awakens the pleasure of making the unknown known and ignites the desire to remember your true self...in every new NOW-moment. There is joy in finding and revealing your hidden self.

Children love peek-a-boo and hide-and-seek because they know that 'revealing the hidden' is just a game to be enjoyed while playing. The point is not to lift the veil for good – the point is to know your true self behind the veil *while* playing with it. Knowing that even when you do not 'see' your true self, it is still there... peeking behind the veil.

55 | *The FUN aspect*
of a limitation
is the creative ACT
it takes to transform it
into FREEDOM.

'In here' and 'out there'

56 | *We do not observe reality,*
we observe our REACTIONS to it.

In other words:
reality is, in essence, neutral.
YOU give it meaning.

Although spending time in the realm of academia gave me opportunities to explore many aspects of my intellect, it also made me painfully aware of the generally accepted 'split' between the 'subjectiveness' of thoughts and the 'objectiveness' of the world outside.

During the years I spent studying art, psychology and communication, I never felt that my or the other students' thoughts truly mattered – unless of course, they were the *'right'* thoughts: confirming an already fixed and 'objective' view of the world outside.

It seems that, at least in the academic realm, the 'objective' reality does not have to 'prove' anything. It simply is. Accepted as it is – as The Truth. I, on the other hand, even though I was one of the best students, had to 'prove' every thought.

The key discoveries of early quantum physics reveal to us that the elemental essence of reality is not an *objective* physical, material reality *'out there.'* Instead, the reality out there, it tells us, is unlimited probabilities and possibilities waiting for a *subjective* consciousness to 'think' them into being.

And yet Western society has not adapted to these scientifically proven facts. Our current worldview – one in which human beings have to adjust and submit to a fixed objective material reality *'out there'* – is undisputedly accepted as the supreme one.

So, how does this worldview affect us? It leaves us with a split-reality experience where *'in here'* and *'out there'* never meet. Where *'out there'* is the only truth and therefore has more authority than *'in here'*. Where *'out there'* is objective, concrete, real and indisputable, whereas *'in here'* is private, lucid, surreal and questionable.

This worldview projects a reality where we seem to live in our subjective *'In-Here-Bubbles'*, aimlessly floating in the objective *'Out-There-Reality'* and only able to respond and react to whatever the *'Out-There-Reality'* throws at us. We feel that we are not in charge of our own reality – because it appears to be conditioned and ruled by unyielding *'out-there'* facts and truths.

It is a reality into which we are born and are compelled to participate in, but cannot change. Here is a suggestion: take a bite of the apple and understand where you are and how your reality works:

57 | *REALITY*
has no meaning of its own.

YOU
give it meaning
by what you
perceive and define
it to be.

CHANGE
your mind
and everything
changes.

Every event, incident or thing that happens in your life is neutral in origin. You define it into existence by giving it *your* meaning. It is your *definition* of the circumstances that colours the experience and gives it a positive or negative charge. You are the subjective consciousness thinking it into being by choosing to observe it.

58 | *The only real and truly objective reality is*
All That Is containing all that is.
Everything else is created and perceived
by focused awareness through a subjective mind.

YOU ('in here') and your reality ('out there') are ONE. Your reality is created by YOU.

YOU matter!

We live in a society that tells us there is an objective reality 'out there' and that we are subjective bystanders simply looking on as it evolves. This makes us believe that we cannot do anything to change reality – that we are powerless and helpless, and all we can do is watch it change.

We have been conditioned to ignore and thus disown our part in the creation of our reality. We nurture the beliefs that our thoughts do not matter and that our emotions are a private matter when it comes to important matter.

YOU are important! YOU matter!

59 | *The more you know*
the immense range
of your own power,
the less others can tap in to it,
and use you.

Own your own power! You are not just a powerless bystander watching your life unfold. YOU are the creator of all that is in your reality. Honour your own power. Trust who you are. Respect yourself.

The dilemma of describing ONE

60

Words are symbols of illusions.
When I speak, I feel the limiting aspect of my words.

Every word is a separation from ONE.
Good or bad is a perspective.
Light or dark is just a game.
Past and future are off the point,
since the only 'point' where I am,
is HERE and NOW.

I try to free my sentences from
the bondage of illusion
by enclosing infinite eternity into a circle of words:
ALL is ONE. One is All That Is. I am ONE.

Am I just a symbol of an illusion?
Am I a word,
a sound,
a thought of all the possible ONES?
What am I?

I am my SELF.
I am ONE consciousness
existing in ONE NOW-moment,
experiencing ONE of the infinite facets of oneness
defined as ME.

The circle closes itself in my mind.
I am ONE.
ONE is All That Is.
ALL is ONE.

The flow of eternal time

61 | *Success is not a question of how much power or money you have acquired. It is a question of how satisfied you are with WHO YOU ARE.*

Do you love your self? Do you love your life? Do you love what you do?

Because, you see, there is joy in abundance. Love is everywhere. Happiness is for free. When you do what you love, abundance always finds a way to find you. Love – in all its shapes, colours and forms – has a magical ability to transcend time and space by opening a 'gate' that connects us to eternity.

Time seems to stop, or at least slow down, in the flow of love and joy. It flies by when we are absorbed in doing something we love, and in that moment we experience agelessness. When one hour feels like five minutes, you have aged five minutes while the rest of the world has aged one hour.

Think about that.

People who love what they do and do what they love look healthy, emanate 'good vibes' and continue to inspire others, even at an old age.

Success, then, is more a question of how much 'time' you choose to spend in eternity by doing what you love. The meaning of success cannot be generalized, because it requires you to know who YOU are. When you choose to do what you love, you express your uniqueness and that, in the end, is why you are here now.

Part 3

Why Understanding the Nature of Your Thoughts Changes Everything

Thoughts matter

62 | *Your thoughts matter*
more than matter
because they create matter.

In our society, we have an odd but persistent belief that the *things* seen, heard, felt, smelled or tasted are *real* while the *consciousness* doing all the seeing, hearing, feeling, smelling and tasting has yet to be discovered and proven to *exist*.

Isn't that strange?

Beliefs

63 | *We often feel limited*
by seemingly external forces.
In reality, we are limited only
by our inner thoughts and beliefs.

Everything you have ever been 'taught' – since the day you were born – about how reality works, resides in your beliefs.

64 | *A belief is simply a thought*
that seems true to YOU.

Beliefs are the things you think about yourself when you are alone and the things you believe and 'know' about your reality. While these might seem like your own creation and feel like a very private matter, most of the things you believe about yourself and your reality are in fact not really created by you. Most of your beliefs, responses, attitudes and behaviours have been imposed on you by society, school, your parents, your peers, books, TV and other media.

The way I see it, negative self-talk is never true and nor is it accurate, because it is often based on false beliefs that are 'suggested' by 'authorities' in your reality. Some of your beliefs *are* true and accurate, but most of them are limiting your thoughts and actions and need reshaping so they fit into your future reality.

For instance, you could believe that people are ignorant. This is a belief that you will not *perceive* as a belief. You will simply see it as a condition of reality. But it is *still* just a belief, albeit a strong one – shaping your view of humanity by blocking out everything that contradicts it.

So if your goal is to make humanity more 'aware', but you keep focusing on 'people's ignorance', you are actually attracting more ignorance and less awareness in your reality. A belief that is holding you back is never true, although it still might *seem* real and true to you.

As I said earlier, one of the most misleading beliefs we have in our society is that our thoughts do not matter. The truth is that thoughts *become* matter. Knowing this, and acting on it, is to transform 'limitations' – beliefs – into freedom. What you believe to be true – good or bad – is nothing more than a belief you can change if it does not serve you.

65

Negative BELIEFS about yourself are ALWAYS false.

Every child is born flawlessly COMPLETE and perfectly PERFECT.

The pliant nature of your beliefs

66 | *When YOU choose to change, everything changes.*

Do you believe that 'life is a struggle' or that 'you must work hard to get what you want in life'? If you do, then *struggle* and *hard work* will keep manifesting in your immediate reality as a negative outcome of that belief.

If your life is not what you want it to be or you feel that you only encounter obstacles, you need to review your beliefs about common, seemingly solid and unquestionable 'truths' such as these. Actually, if you want to make a change in your reality, examining your beliefs and unquestioned 'truths' should be number one on your 'to do' list.

So, what *is* a limiting belief and how do you find and eliminate it?

You are processing information about your reality literally *all* the time. Since thoughts are energy and a belief is a cluster of many repetitive thoughts, a more focused or 'dense' energy emits from the belief, attracting and accumulating other thoughts and emotions of the same vibrational frequency.

Left unattended, a limiting belief grows stronger: it gains power and solidifies itself perpetually. To stop it from overpowering your perception of reality, you must consciously choose to change the frequency of your thoughts and emotions by starting to question the validity of the limiting belief.

A simple way to detect a limiting belief is to focus on your emotions. Things that make you feel unworthy, powerless or frightened are *all* generated by limiting beliefs – keeping you imprisoned in your own mind by leaving you feeling 'not good enough' or 'small'. A limiting belief triggers fear and worry and more importantly, if left unquestioned, it soon disguises itself as a 'true' aspect of reality.

Know the truth:

67 | *Everything in your reality*
that drains you of power or energy
is based on FALSE beliefs.

We are ALL born amazing.
Everything else is conditioned behaviour.

All negative beliefs that are
diminishing YOU, are thus untrue.

Beliefs are rooted in emotions and imagination. They are seldom purely intellectual. So if you want to change the beliefs behind your thoughts and actions, you have to look at the feelings that are accompanying them and the imaginative ideas that keep reinforcing them. Limiting beliefs always hide behind draining negative feelings about yourself. They work like an underlying programme, selecting the negative information while filtering out the positive information.

68 | *To change the programme,*
you must actively look
for the positive information.

In any given situation, always choose
the best possible perspective.

The plain truth is that what you believe, you perceive. Your beliefs create your reality. Seventy per cent or more of your beliefs are subconscious because they were created in your childhood before you could question them. This means they manifest *automatically* and therefore give the impression of being a solid part of your reality because you are not *aware* of their existence. You only perceive their result.

You cannot change your beliefs as long as you perceive their result as 'solid' reality outside of yourself. To change them, you must first understand and truly accept that *you* are the one creating everything in your reality, based on what you believe to be true. The good news is that we are never born with beliefs. A belief always comes from the outside.

69 | *Beliefs are only ideas and viewpoints*
about the way reality is structured
and how it works.
They are not written in stone.

Beliefs can be altered, changed, modified, erased, replaced or amplified. By YOU. All you have to do is see the pliant illusion behind all the negative beliefs. Your source is unconditional, accepting, inclusive and embracing. The negative is a necessary illusion in the fabric of the physical Universe so you can exercise your free will and consciously choose the positive alternative.

Choosing the most positive and beneficial interpretation of reality and everything in it, is a rarely understood and seldom-used privilege of being here.

70
*If it feels GOOD,
trust it as TRUE.*

*If it feels BAD,
discharge it as NOT TRUE.*

The same goes for your reality. It manifests your deepest thoughts and strongest beliefs about yourself. When you change a belief, you change your perspective and thus your point of view. Since YOU are the observer and creator of your reality, it has no other option but to change according to the viewpoint YOU choose.

71
*You are always creating:
either through positive beliefs and desires
or negative beliefs and fears.*

The choice is yours.

*When YOU choose to change,
your reality must change accordingly.
It simply has no other choice.*

Ego

72 | *Ego is an important aspect of being a human being.*

In itself, ego is actually not a bad thing.

There is a common belief about the ego: we are taught that ego is not good for us and that we need to become spiritual and one with our source – All That Is – in order to know who we truly are.

But the way I see it, this is not how physical reality really works. I see ego as a neutral 'tool' that simply has the task of 'separating' something out from All That Is and defining this 'something's' boundaries or limits. And it does so for a reason – in order for All That Is to experience itself as me or you or anyone else, it needs to focus consciousness in one point. Ego is that focusing tool, enclosing a central point of activity for your spirit to 'inhabit'.

So in itself, ego is not a bad thing. It is an important aspect of being a human being, enabling a soul to focus itself into a body and experience physical reality. Without your ego, you would not know where you end and outer reality begins. Ego helps you define YOU. It is when humans forget that ego is just a 'focusing tool' and ego becomes their *prime* or *only identity*, that it turns into a negative force perpetuating fear and hate.

Initially, then, ego is not a negative thing. It is a neutral 'device' that focuses you into being YOU. And furthermore, your ego contains your specific desires, wishes and passions. All of which are important for the spiritual evolution of the human species.

But ego needs to be balanced with the knowledge of our infinite, eternal spiritual source. Our source – or All That Is – is inclusive, inviting, embracing, infinite and limitless. Ego, on the other hand, is separating, excluding, defining, finite and limiting. It has to be, in order for you to be focused on being YOU.

Our source is unconditional acceptance and love, but if we focus ourselves too much on that, we become less distinguished in the physical reality. Ego is based on restrictions. Its primary function is to distinguish YOU as 'separate' from All That Is and to define your essential qualities, limits and boundaries. This is why ego contains all your personal desires, wishes, goals, passions, wants and needs.

Your ego will tell you your specific take on this physical reality – your specific wants and needs. It will tell you what you enjoy and what you love in this physical reality. In short, ego contains your desires. And isn't that what life actually is all about? Exploring what you love, exploring what you find interesting, exploring your passions? If you silence your ego (your focus-point) and become more of All That Is, you miss the point of being in a physical reality.

Your infinite soul wants to explore what it is like to have limitations, what it is like to have a body. If we just dream about the spiritual world or getting out of this body, we miss the point of being here altogether. And we fail to see the beauty of having a physical life.

A couple of years ago I saw a German movie that affected me tremendously – it is called *Wings of Desire*. The story is about an eternal angel who oversees human activity and secretly dreams of becoming a human being. The movie reminded me of the incredible beauty to be found in everyday things. I mean things that we usually take for granted: the smell of a newspaper, the taste of coffee, the touch of a hand, the wind in our hair, the rain on our face....

The angel had the privilege of time – or more correctly, he had the privilege of no-time, because he was eternal. Yet he was unable to fully enjoy his being because he had no 'body' through which he could experience physical reality.

The story made me understand how privileged we actually are to be in this reality. I realized that my spirit is focused in time and space for a reason – a *physical* reason. It is here because of an experience it cannot have in the spiritual realm: that of being *me*, or *you* or *anyone* here. The ego becomes the tool that focuses All That Is into me, into you and into every single ONE of us.

73 | *Physical reality is about creating BALANCE between the eternally entangled polarities of mind and matter, body and soul, ego and spirit.*

Stay creative and open

74 | *Things do not happen TO you.*
They happen THROUGH you.

You are the co-creator
of everything in your reality.

Imagine a soap bubble. Children are perceived as pure, vulnerable and delicate because when they are born, the boundary or 'veil' between '*in here*' and '*out there*' is as transparent, sheer and beautiful as the colourful surface of a soap bubble.

During the early years of our lives we do not see any boundaries between '*in here*' and '*out there*'. Without thinking about it, we seamlessly interact between them, creating magic in our timeless reality, just for the joy of it: retracting our '*In-Here-Bubble*', then expanding it, bursting it and re-creating it. Over and over again.

As we grow up, our beliefs about ourselves and our reality become increasingly rigid and concrete, creating a hardening of the translucent and evanescent surface of our '*In-Here-Bubble*'. The more we accept others' opinions, beliefs and attitudes about ourselves and the world around us, the harder the bubble's surface becomes. Until finally, it disconnects us from our dreamlike, innately co-creative relationship with the '*out-there*' reality.

We become lonely travellers in the fabric of the Universe, unable to remember the original dreamlike lucidity and sheerness of our *'In-Here-Bubble'*. We forget that we are co-creators of our reality and that our reality will provide everything we believe to be true.

To re-soften the surface of our *'In-Here-Bubble'* and expand it, we need to be creative and open again, like children. But what does this actually mean?

To remember the feeling of careless playing and enjoying, please repeat after me:

75

I EXPECT
joy and fun.

I KNOW
that things always
work out for me.

I TRUST
my flow.

Now read the lines again, only this time, really 'taste' the words in your mouth. Feel their energy in your body and allow their meaning to heighten your frequency. In this way, you can daydream and play a more joyful reality into existence. For what is reality, if not a shared interactive dream believed into existence?

One morning, my then seven-year-old son said to me: 'What if everything is a dream? I am a dream... you are a dream... Dad is a dream... I am so glad that we are dreaming the *same* dream!'

Negativity and struggle

76 | *Life does not have to be*
'hard work' or a 'struggle'.

Be conscious of WHAT you are doing,
and WHY you are doing it.

That is all.

Are you willing to explore unknown territory in order to become who you truly are, by daring to ask yourself uncomfortable questions? Someone once asked me an intriguing question about struggle and negativity I think many of us would like to master by understanding:

> *'I have been on a journey of self-discovery most of my*
> *life – never taking the status quo as the way. If there*
> *was a means of going upstream, I always found it...*
>
> *... but recently, I have realized that regardless of how*
> *hard I have tried, all these years, to direct my thoughts*
> *and to focus on positivity, my subconscious seems*
> *to be driven by fear and negativity. Where do these*
> *negative thoughts originate? How do I get rid of them?'*

What caught my attention was the way the person described the 'drive' to be different, and the battle between positive and negative thoughts. But also the result of that struggle – the subconscious mind being driven by fear. In order to answer the question, I would like to recapture some of my thoughts about the structure of reality.

As I explained earlier, the way I see it, as souls we chose (i.e. before birth) to explore physical life in a reality based on polarities. This basically means that as human beings we live in a physical reality in which there is an equal amount of +/−, light/darkness, love/fear balancing as possibilities and probabilities that are waiting for our 'awareness' to choose them from the infinite quantum field (All That Is, Source, the Universe, God).

The tricky part is that what our awareness 'chooses' is not always based on our thoughts and our 'strong will', but rather on our true *intention* and deepest *beliefs* about ourselves and our reality.

We are beings made of vibrating energy – as is everything else in our Universe – so the only 'thing' differentiating me from you or sand from water is the vibrational frequency of that energy. Every thought, emotion or thing has its own unique frequency. For example, love is a higher frequency than fear.

So, what has that to do with our question? Well, everything... because in this 'reality-creating-mechanism,' what you *put out* is what you *get back* – your frequency is mirrored back to you by the quantum field. And the quantum field does not make mistakes. It unconditionally reflects back to you a perfect match in frequency. In other words, it is our innermost *intentions* that set the frequency of our being. The frequency is then perfectly matched by the quantum field and ultimately perceived by us as solid reality, things, relationships, circumstances, thoughts and feelings.

The 'invitation' for negative thoughts in the question above comes from the underlying belief that 'hard work' always pays off. But hard work equals success only if you love what you do. Otherwise the struggle, imbedded in the concept of 'hard work', sets us in the low frequencies of uncertainty, negativity and worry, which can be summed up in one word: FEAR.

Fear is a low frequency. It is the opposing force to LOVE and to every positive thing we strive and struggle for by 'working hard'.

We are conditioned by Western society and culture to believe that we will not 'get anywhere in life' unless we work hard. So there is a misconception in our current belief system around what it takes to be successful. The implication is that, without struggle, there can be no results. As the saying goes, 'no pain, no gain'.

We think it is good to fight against the current in the river of life because we believe that it will differentiate us from the rest of the people. But to my way of thinking, it is actually the other way around. Literally speaking. In order to differentiate YOU from the rest, you need to relax and go with *your* flow. Because everyone else is 'doing their best', 'working hard', or 'pouring their heart out' in order to stay where they are by clinging on to a branch or a rock.

Those who really believe in the idea that 'hard work always pays off' even force themselves to move upstream. This is an action that uses up a lot of energy while keeping us in constant 'fighting-the-flow-mode'. What it will not do is get us to the relaxed, positive and calm 'place' we are looking for upstream.

Consider this: in order for you to establish *your* flow in the river of life, you need to relax and allow yourself to connect to your source – which is an 'ocean' of unconditional love, compassion, expansion and self-love – and match *that* frequency. Struggle is a much lower frequency than your source. The negative thoughts are just reminders that you need to change your frequency. They are actually telling you that you are out of alignment with your true self and that you need to:

77 | *Breathe in your unbound soul:*
there is no need for control.
Act less, observe more and grow.
Relax and surrender to your flow.

You might ask, 'Isn't surrendering to the flow the same as giving up? After all, "only dead fish go with the flow."' And my answer would be: 'What has that to do with you? YOU are the river. YOU are the *flow*.'

Besides:

78 | *Surrender is not the same as giving up.*
It is more a matter of letting go of struggle
and giving in to the synchronistic flow
of manifestation.

So, trust your self. Let go of the branches and the rocks. Stop wasting time fighting your self, struggling upstream. Allow yourself to go with your flow, because following your flow is the same as trusting the river of life – your source – to take you where you need to go. Do not be afraid. What you will find, following your flow, is just more of YOU.

79

The Universe does not create through 'hard work' and 'struggle'. Trust and FLOW are the modes of manifestation. Relax and follow your BLISS.

Worry and daydreaming

80 | *Worry and daydreaming are different aspects of the same thing: your creative imagination.*

Worrying creates blueprints of what you do not want in your future.

Daydreaming creates blueprints of what you do want in your future.

Worrying leaves you powerless, drained and tired because it seems to be driven by 'outside' forces, and therefore gives the impression of being 'out of your control'. It is like having your mind hijacked by someone using your imagination to project images of worst-case scenarios and outcomes, without you being able to stop it.

Daydreaming, on the other hand, leaves you empowered, satisfied and energized because it feels as if *you* are the one feeding your mind with positive images of your joys, desires and wants. *You* seem to be in control of the outcome.

The way I see it, you are using the same source – your imagination – in both cases, but getting completely different results. The reason for this is that your reality acts like a 'field' outside of you, reflecting your deepest beliefs and thoughts about yourself. Since this field works as a 3D mirror, it 'obeys' everything you 'tell' it to do. So if you focus your awareness on worry, it will give you more 'images', 'ideas' and 'results' for worry in the form of solid reality.

You might be thinking *What kind of mechanism is this? Why would it reflect back a bad thing that I don't want in my reality?* The answer is: because it is unconditional and neutral. It behaves like a mirror. It will not argue with you or try to change your mind – it is all accepting, and above all, it respects your free will. If you smile, the mirror smiles back. If you frown, the mirror frowns back.

You are the one choosing to smile – sending the smile and receiving it back. Everything you think comes back to you. You are the sender and the receiver. Your imagination determines your reality. Your thoughts, feelings and deepest beliefs are reflected in this field 'outside' of you. It creates the reality you imagine.

Actually, this is the meaning behind the saying 'Be careful what you wish for'. The word 'wish' could easily be replaced with 'think about', 'believe', 'focus your mind on', 'dwell on' or 'talk about'.

Know this:

81 | *Worrying is unintentional creation of your future.*
      | *Daydreaming is intentional creation of your future.*

The choice is always yours.

Trying to understand the concept of unintentional creation of reality – to grasp its negative aspects and the fact that we actually have a choice – used to keep me up at night. My thoughts would go something like this:

If I am the one generating my reality, then how exactly am I doing this? I understand how I create the positive things, because they are what I deliberately want. They are conscious choices in the sense that I have daydreamed, desired and wished them into existence.

I have focused my awareness on them, and so I have made them consciously. But what about the negative things? I mean, why would I 'want' negative things in my reality?

The answer is: I don't.

The key to this question is very simple: your reality answers *all your beliefs*, unconditionally. Worrying is like a constant negative prayer or mantra, generating a reality that you fear. And this is an important thing to understand – you create your reality with what you imagine and *believe to be true* about yourself. The Universe answers *exactly* and unconditionally to that *specific* frequency.

In a sense, daydreaming is like creating good 'memories' of something yet to come. When you daydream, you deliberately tune your frequency in to your desires, by creating inner pictures of your future self. It can be likened to remembering the past. Only while daydreaming or visualizing, you are 'remembering' good 'memories' of the future.

82 | *As an emotionally strong memory*
brings the past into your present,
so daydreaming draws
a new future into your present
by shifting your frequency in the now.

When you daydream, you visualize a perfect 'movie', with all the details of your wishes, dreams and desires in your mind. Enjoying your daydream is the easiest way to change your frequency on demand because it tunes you in to joy, anticipation and hope. This, in turn, speeds up the manifestation process and allows otherwise invisible opportunities into your reality.

83 | *Use your free will*
to choose what
you daydream
into this reality.

Part 4

Why Finding
Your Flow
Changes
Everything

Change is the only constant

84 | *Stop worrying.*

*Everything in the Universe
is in constant change.*

Nothing stays the same.

*Enjoy the movement.
Enjoy the dance.
Enjoy the surprise.*

Sometimes we choose to remain in a situation just because it feels more familiar than opening up to something new. We feel safer staying in 'the known', even if it might be bad, rather than exposing ourselves to 'the unknown', even if it might bring us joy. Why are we so reluctant to change, and often afraid of the new, when our natural state of being is to seek joy and to trust everything that 'the unknown' holds for us?

As children, we could not resist the funny rush of surprise we felt when trying new things because we knew intuitively that we are here on Earth for the joy of exploring physical reality by collecting moments of exciting new experiences. But as we grew up, we gradually became *'Consumers-Of-Things'* – forgetting our original soul purpose as *'Collectors-Of-Experiences'*. Now we want to explore new things, but we do not want to experience the uncertainty of change.

So, how do you explore something without being willing to change yourself with the experience? The answer is that you don't explore, you don't expand and you don't evolve. You simply exist. Habitually.

> 'And then the day came, when the risk to remain tight in a bud was more painful than the risk it took to Blossom.'
>
> ANAÏS NIN

Nature does not avoid change. Nature embraces and allows transformation because it works in unison with the Universe and the divine law of change, rebirth, renewal, revival and new beginnings. Everything simply flows, perfectly choreographed in an intricate dance of speed and calmness, light and dark, life and death.

Breathing in... trust.

Breathing out... patience.

Breathing in... out. In... and... out.

Like waves on a shore, for infinity, nature 'knows' that change is an entangled part of being; that every 'NOW-moment' holds the element of change.

Take, for instance, the concept of yin and yang. It is the expression of perfect harmony and yet it contains the aspect of change and chaos. Have you noticed the small white and black dots in the perfectly balanced pattern of its symbol? They are important reminders of life's transitory qualities, of the simple truth that all things eventually change.

You cannot breathe in without breathing out. If you hold your breath for too long it becomes painful and you must release the pressure by breathing out. Letting it go. Allowing the new.

Here is an esoteric truth:

85 | *Change is the only constant.*
Everything else is in constant change.

Nothing in the physical reality stays the same. Resisting this fundamental force is meaningless because the resistance itself will change you – moulding you into someone you do not want to be. As the English philosopher Alan W. Watts said: 'The only way to make sense out of change is to plunge into it, move with it and join the dance.'

But what seems to hold us back from 'joining the dance' is the fear of not knowing how to move in the 'right' way, and of 'dancing to the wrong music'. So we hesitate and we fear change. And it is a painful fear because it comes from a persistent doubt in our reality.

Our perception of the world around us is rooted in the conditioned belief that we live in a cold and harsh Universe. A Universe that presents us with a solid reality in which we are supposed to exist under already created circumstances and in which our lives have little or no significance. It is a worldview that makes us believe there is a subjective and lonely *'inside'* – without the power to influence anything – looking out on an objective and all-powerful mechanistic *'outside'*.

Here is an alternative thought: cutting-edge science, along with ancient knowledge, tells us that there are no 'real' boundaries between things – between *'inside'* and *'outside'*. Everything is connected and needs an *observer* to exist.

So, welcome to a reality in which *you* are in a creative *relationship* with everything 'around' you. You are in a creative relationship with the Universe. Actually, the Universe is your *partner* in creation. You are the Observer. The Universe is the abundant Provider, patiently waiting to joyously expand within your desires, wishes and thoughts.

Author Anaïs Nin's rosebud is pushed into bloom by forces much stronger than fear, doubt or worry. The life force behind this unfolding and opening up 'act' is a desire to become more than you are: to expand your self beyond all limitations in search of new experiences.

When you open up, you face more light, you embrace more air, you consume more water – and the rosebud knows that it is the only way to grow. Actually, it knows that it is the only way to *live*. So, face the sun. Let it remind you of who you are. Take pleasure in breathing. Allow the flow of change and enjoy the surprise.

86

You are in a creative relationship with everything 'around' you.
The Universe is the abundant Provider.
You are the Receiver.

The Universe is your partner in Creation.
What you ask for, the Universe will provide.

Change is your natural state of being

There is a difference between *making* change and *allowing* change.

The dominant perspective in our society on how to grow or make transitions from one state of being to another – be it a global organization or a single person – is mainly about how to *take action* and how to *make change* happen. The way we use words when we talk about change indicates, on a subconscious level of our collective mind, that in order to make any kind of change, force is required and active action is necessary.

But humans are habitual beings who do not like to feel 'forced' into new patterns and behaviours. This is the reason why speaking about change in terms of 'action' and 'making' creates quiet resistance and involuntary inertia, before we even start the process of changing.

If we shift perspective and look at change as a natural and inevitable part of reality – which, by the way, is the prevailing state in nature – then creating real and lasting change becomes more a question of how to *allow* change to happen, rather than *make* it happen. The way I see it, as a species we are not reluctant to change per se. We just don't like the act of *making* it.

Making a change indicates that it takes an effort or use of force, which we subconsciously interpret as a thing that requires energy from us. *Allowing* change, on the other hand, signifies effortlessness and ease – giving us time to accept and embrace it, while at the same time being invigorated with energy by it. In both cases change occurs, only with very different results.

So, how do we create situations and circumstances where *allowing* change is as natural as breathing in and out? Leaders who understand the subtle, yet very powerful, quantum energies at play when people interact, know intuitively that in order to create smooth transitions from one state to another, they first need to 'mimic' nature by creating a 'culture of allowing' in the workplace.

Let me give you an example. When we allow 'mistakes' to be a part of the learning process – by using 'failure' as feedback, which helps us grow and get even better at what we are doing – fear is eliminated and creativity unleashed. Nourishing creativity in this way allows imagination to play freely, which inevitably allows change to simply happen. Just as effortlessly as nature *allows* the slow, steady and perpetuating movement of change to renew and invigorate her.

We are the ones creating our own reality by how we interpret and perceive it. As you already know, reality needs an observer to exist – an observer who *chooses* what he/she wants to perceive. So in other words, what we *choose* to perceive, we create. And yes, change *is* constant and thus inevitable, but we are the ones choosing the *type* and *quality* of that change. And that means it is up to us. It is about what we choose. We cannot avoid the change, but we sure can point it in the 'right' direction.

87 | *Like martial arts masters*
we need to 'dance' with creation
by allowing what we like
and diverting what we do not like
in the flow of constant change.

In this way, change becomes not just a goal to reach, but a *tool* for you to *use* so you can grow in your consciousness and see more facets of who YOU are. It becomes something you actually *are* in the present moment, and not just something you plan for and make happen in the future. Instead of *doing*, change becomes a natural state of *being*.

Here are some simple things to follow if you want to create an atmosphere in which change is smoothly allowed, without the friction of doubt and resistance:

88 | *Know your self.*
Trust your self.
Interact honestly with others.
Focus on the solutions.
Always look for the best in others.

This is a very good and easy way to start an avalanche of positive change, without any effort.

Do what YOU love

89 | *Successful people do what they love, not what they are told to do.*

Successful people follow their excitement, no matter what. They resist negative suggestions from others, no matter what. They are committed to their desires and passions, no matter what.

Success looks easy because it actually *is* easy. When you know what you love and stick to doing that no matter what, no problem is too big to handle and no obstacle too big to overcome. The key is knowing *what* you love to do. In order to discover this, you need to know *who* you are. Because if you do not know *who* YOU are, how will you know *what* YOU love?

It might feel like a catch-22 situation, but when you think about it, it is really very simple. *Who* you are and *what* you love are actually one and the same thing. YOU are what you LOVE. You are not in this reality by accident: you are here to fearlessly explore all your desires and passions. Life becomes a struggle the moment you start ignoring what you love by setting aside your passions or dreams in favour of what someone else thinks is 'right' for you to do.

90 | *Doing what you 'should'*
will make you average.

Doing what you love,
no matter what,
makes you outstanding.

Emotional pain and uncertainty can enter your mind only when you allow 'outer' reality to get under your skin and tell you what is 'right' and 'wrong' in your reality. Allowing others' thoughts, beliefs and values to 'dictate' how you think and act – particularly when they are *not in alignment* with who you are – only creates inertia in YOU.

It takes valuable energy to fight this 'inner battle' between your true self and the 'outer' beliefs of a different frequency than your own. Successful people know intuitively that the only fulfilling path through life is pursuing your dreams, no matter what.

This is so because:

91 | *Doing what you LOVE*
will always reveal
the fearless, illuminated spirit
that YOU truly are...
... even in the darkest hour.

Your true self is at its most beneficial frequency when you are doing what you love. This is because LOVE is your source – love is who you are. It is where YOU originate. It is your core. Pursuing your dreams while doing what you love is not just one of the highest missions in your life, it is also your birthright.

Letting fear stop you from using this incredible birthright would be an awful waste of time, energy and space. So, just do what you love, no matter what!

92 | *LOVE is the primary pattern in the fabric of the Universe. Everything else is secondary.*

'Right' knowledge

93 | *Knowledge is not power.*
The RIGHT knowledge is power.

Knowledge has nothing to do with quantity and everything to do with quality. What is the use in having lots of knowledge about useless things?

So what, then, is the *right* knowledge? All information that sets YOUR spirit free is the right knowledge – knowledge that connects you to your core. Everything else is conditioning that restricts you from expanding and evolving.

Birthrights, freedoms and needs

94 | *Basic human BIRTHRIGHTS:*
clean water, clean air,
nourishing food, a home,
free speech, free thought, FREEDOM.

Basic human FREEDOMS:
The pursuit of happiness.
Doing what you love.
Being who you are.
Using your time as you wish.

Basic human NEEDS:
LOVE, privacy, eye CONTACT,
a touch, a smile,
respect, a second CHANCE,
to be HEARD, to be SEEN.

Part 5

Why Understanding the Nature of Fear Changes Everything

What is fear?

95 | *The two faces of FEAR:*
one instantly saving your life,
the other slowly killing you.

See the CHOICE.

Fear is something that can alter our perception of reality in many different ways. There are two kinds: one acute, life-saving *direct* fear, which heightens our awareness, and one slowly sneaking *indirect* fear, which lowers our awareness. The same basic emotion, fear, produces completely different results, depending on how it enters our reality and how we cope with it.

Being in the midst of a car accident, in fear of losing your life, will heighten your awareness, sharpen your perception of time and space and activate your thinking and actions. This is an example of acute, life-saving direct fear. The adrenaline in your bloodstream will make you alert and quick thinking. When the immediate danger is over, you will have time to recover by resting your mind and letting your body regulate the adrenaline back to normal levels.

By contrast, being perpetually reminded of negative things in your reality – for example, the notion that you are 'not good enough', or the prospect of losing your job or fear of the 'war on terror' – will lower your awareness, narrow your perception of your options and stagnate your sense of time and space.

This is an example of slowly sneaking indirect fear. The initial adrenaline in your blood will eventually turn into toxins that not only slow down your thinking and stop you from taking actions aligned with who you truly are, but actually cause decay in your body.

Slowly sneaking indirect fear is an illness generator. It triggers dis-harmonic frequencies in your body that, while disguising themselves as a 'normal' ingredient in your everyday reality, effectively reduce the quality of your life over time.

The good news is that you can limit the effect of slowly sneaking indirect fear by actively choosing not to let your surroundings influence you. For instance, your reality is not as fearful as the news media want you to believe – look at your immediate surroundings, look at the nature around you. Nothing needs to be feared. Everything is as it is – like an intricate dance slowly changing between stillness and motion. That's all.

96

Your surroundings influence you.
Turn off your TV.
Do not gossip.
Do not read trashy magazines.

Another quick way of getting rid of negative influences from your surroundings is to consciously select your 'friends' and the people with whom you interact. Sometimes you need to simply say 'no' to others and 'yes' to YOU, so that you can allow yourself time to recreate peace in your mind and body.

97 | *Choose consciously:*
WHO you spend time with.
HOW you spend time.
WHAT you ALLOW.

YOU are real. Fear is not

98 | *Fear makes us conform*
to things we usually would not.

Know this:
YOU are real.
Fear is not!

In our model of society, a culture of fear seems to be created, promoted and conveyed to us by a minority of people in positions of power. These 'fear dealers' construct crisis after crisis and wage wars on terror, crime or drugs – pushing their own political agendas by using the language of stress and fear.

Meanwhile, the corporate media perpetuate this fabricated fear by constantly reminding us of the dangers, risks and horrors that await us just around the corner. This is further nurtured by an entertainment business supplying us with certain 'fear-fixes' through blockbusting 'end-of-the-world' films and violent TV series and video games.

Have you ever wondered why fear seems to be the driving force in our society? Fear is a major tool for controlling people's perception of the reality they live in. The mechanism is simple: fear triggers our self-preservation by creating an illusion of danger. The minute we buy into this illusion, we become citizens of 'survival-world'. It literally catapults us into a mass agreed-upon insanity where ignorance or mental blankness is the 'foundation' and black-or-white thinking the 'norm'.

This is so because:

99 | *Fear lowers your frequency,*
limiting your field of vibration
and thus obscuring your perception
of your reality.

Fear diminishes your connection to your brain and to your heart. The fear-illusion disconnects you from your soul-source, limits your access to the emotional centres of your brain and destabilizes your intellectual balance.

Like a vampire, fear drains your body of energy, leaving behind only your nodding, conscientious shadow. Controlling people's perception of reality through the fear-illusion is the simplest way to gain social control and power because people cannot stand upright when they are down on their knees, trembling. You need to be able to see through the fear-illusion and have the strength to get up first.

Here is a starter:

100 | *To reclaim your:*
MIND – stop paying attention to 'news'!
VISION – stop watching TV!
INTEGRITY – stop falling prey to 'drama'!

101

*Your reality is not what
the news media tell you it is.*

Look outside and see for yourself.

*Remember:
Fear is an illusion.
YOU are not.*

See the smiling people, the blue sky and the laughing children in the park. It is all there. All you have to do is see it! The American author Christopher Moore sums it up in one short sentence: 'Children see magic because they look for it.'

And that's the trick! It is not naïve, childish, blindly optimistic, illogical, irresponsible or stupid to actively choose the focus of your attention. Because what you focus your attention on becomes your reality. If fear, worry or doubt occupy your mind and heart, you are under the spell of the fear-illusion and that is the reality you are co-creating.

Do not take this lightly. You believe *everything* you think. Make sure that what you say to yourself really comes from *your* source *within* and not from someone else's beliefs and interests from *without*.

102

*Nothing has a greater impact
on how your life unfolds
than your thoughts.*

Nothing!

*THINK
good,
abundant,
loving,
creative
THOUGHTS.*

103

*Life is precious.
Pay attention to nature, love,
understanding and beauty.*

Do you see the magic NOW?

Change fear of rejection into power

104 | *Fear of rejection is a REMINDER of your self-worth.*

It is telling you that you are giving away your power to an EXTERNAL source.

Fear of rejection is a negative belief which, when looked at from a different perspective, actually reveals something positive to you about your self-worth. It is allowing you to see that you are giving away your own power to an *external* source. It exposes a subconscious limiting belief within you and in doing so, gives you an *opportunity to reclaim your power.* Just by becoming aware of the subconscious belief and by recognizing its underlying energy, you can change its structure and negative effect.

The underlying belief that feeds the fear of rejection is the conviction that other people's opinions are more valuable than your own. The externalization of power occurs in the false but very common assumption that what others think and feel matters more than your own thoughts and feelings. Because you intuitively know that you *can* control what *you* think, but you cannot control what *others* think.

The assumption implies that if you just do things the 'right' way, it will please the others and through appreciation they will give you the value you need. The uncertainty this creates sets you in a frequency of fear because it forces you to expend valuable energy and time trying to predict an outcome by second-guessing, speculating and 'deciphering' the needs and wants of *others*.

The truth is:

105 | *The more you try*
to control the outcome,
the more fear is evoked,
and the less you enjoy
what you are doing.

The outcome or result never depends on forces *outside* of you. It is true that you cannot control others, but you can control how their energy *affects* you. Because you see, rejection can wound only when *you allow* it to – when your beliefs are in *subconscious agreement* with what is said about you or done to you.

The truth – the *only* truth – is that you are a fearless soul. Regardless of what others think about you.

106 | *YOU are the sole DEFINER*
of your own VALUE.
Do not let anyone tell you otherwise.

Stop waiting for others to validate YOU.
Your own approval is all you need.

It is *your* life. You are the owner of *everything* in it. The only validation you need is your own! Being aware of this absolute, indisputable truth gives you the power to reclaim your fundamental birthright to always be yourself, no matter what.

So, take a position of Zen calmness and let the false belief disintegrate by reminding yourself of your divine origin and of who you truly are.

107 | *Fear is an illusion.*
YOU are REAL.

Fear is a liar

108

Fear is a liar, telling us to 'stand back' and 'shut up' when in truth we need to stand up and speak out.

Fear is an impostor, portraying us as 'small' when in truth we are infinite spirits with no limits beyond the illusion of time and space.

Fear is a trickster, defining us as 'powerless' when in truth all the power we will ever need was ours at birth.

Negativity and Source

109 | *No matter how bad you feel,*
you can never be 'cut off' from
your unconditionally loving SOURCE.

It is ALWAYS within YOU.

Sadness is there to remind you
that you are out of alignment
with your source.

Many of us have become so used to being uncomfortable in our lives, in our bodies and in our thoughts, that being uncomfortable has paradoxically become the new 'comfort zone'. Instead of actively seeking happiness and joy, we hide from life by occupying our mind with strategies for how to avoid stress and fear.

Everything comfortable has become the scary 'unknown' outside our uncomfortable 'comfort zone' of sadness, fear, stress or worry. We 'boost' each other's 'uncomfortableness' by consistently talking about our fears, worries and problems – thus confirming our 'victim-state-of-mind' as the only reality.

It has become more acceptable to share our obstacles and shortcomings with others than to share our joys and positivity. Why is that?

110

Never reinforce negative thoughts and feelings by repeatedly talking about them.

What you believe, think and speak, you create.

Have you ever wondered why movies containing misery, stress, pain, violence, hate, war and suffering are often regarded as more realistic than those featuring abundance, joy, love, happiness and happy endings? Why does the negative seem more 'real' to us? Why are we more 'comfortable' with the negative? Because we are conditioned to be.

News about accidents, acts of violence, war, conflict, problems, death and fear are continually broadcast, suggesting there is a dangerous reality *'out there'*. These constant reminders about the dangers that surround us set us in a frequency of doubt.

If the world *'out there'* is dangerous and yet we allow ourselves to be happy *'in here'*, then our reality might reject us as naïve – or even worse, as 'not real'. So it feels safer to be in a negative state of mind because it corresponds with the frequency 'outside'. If we feel happy 'inside', our intuition tells us that going out in the 'real' world is bound to change our frequency. Being happy and losing the feeling hurts more than staying negative and maintaining the status quo. Staying in a negative frequency at least gives us an illusion of some kind of control and gives us a feeling of belonging somewhere. It is actually a survival strategy, albeit a very bad one.

In order to change your thoughts from 'survive' to 'thrive', you need to know that there is a *good* reason why negativity exists. Your source is unconditional love and joy. Negativity serves as a contrast to your source. It is helping you define who you truly are by showing you what you are *not*.

It is in the contrast between what you perceive as 'good' or 'bad' that you mark out the boundaries of your true self. Every time you experience negativity, you learn something new about yourself.

111 | *Without darkness there is no light.*
Sometimes you must face
what you are NOT,
in order to understand
what you ARE.

112 | *How are you defining yourself?*
Through fear or through love?
Are you focusing more on
avoiding fear in your everyday life
than on seeking joy and love?

The truth is that the negative is as real as the positive. This is a universal law of the physical reality we live in. Remember: you cannot avoid the negative stuff out there because on a quantum level of reality, we reside in a Universe of polarity. Which means that where there is darkness, where there is black and where there is a minus, an equal amount of light, white and plus must also be present.

The beauty of this dualism is that the polarity exists so you can exercise your free will to choose and there is knowledge and growth in every choice. The quantum field (All That Is, Source, the Universe, God) is always unconditionally responding to your frequency, so it is up to you to find the positive side in the negative occupancy.

In fact, it is your responsibility to actively seek the brighter side of *all* the obstacles and problems you encounter. Every time you feel that your outer reality lowers its frequency, take it as a signal to *raise your* frequency.

113 | *You have to be the light in the darkness.*
You have to be the love in the hate.
You have to be the calmness in the storm.
You have to be the courage in the fear.

And by this, define your true self.

114 | *We live in an abundant Universe*
with plenty for everyone,
yet most of us feel
a persistent sense of lack.

Gratitude allows abundance.

The change you want is just one thought
away – and that thought is within YOU.

Negative feelings such as fear or sadness are only a reminder that you are out of sync with your source, which is unconditional love and joy in abundance. It is reminding you that you should BE unconditional love by unconditionally loving yourself first. It is your soul saying: 'Be your true self! Get back in alignment with your source.'

115 | *There is*
no movement
without stillness,
no sound
without silence,
no light
without darkness
and no ME
without YOU.

Come closer

116

Fear is a veil through which
you cannot see.
Calm yourself –
just breathe with me.
In and out. Rest your heart.
Know that you and I were never apart.

Fear is a veil through which
you cannot see.
Come closer –
just stand with me.
Feel your true power and open your mind.
Look beyond fear, for you are no longer blind.

Fear is just an illusion –
can you see?
Just lift it off and set yourself free.
LOVE reveals what fear conceals.
Let fear go, peacefully.

Part 6

Why Imagination Is Your Tool of Creation

Source of creativity

117 | *We are all born*
unique and AMAZING,
curious and FEARLESS.

Remember the feeling?

If you want to spend time with the truly enlightened ones, go to a park, sit under a tree and watch the children play. Just by observing them we can be inspired to remember who we truly are and why we are here.

Children are amazing! They seem to know all the important things that grown-ups appear to have forgotten. They see magic where grown-ups seek logic, and they do not fear change, because they seek the funny rush of surprise. Children know that we are all here for the joy of exploring, so their primary goal is to seek happiness and have fun. They seem to be effortlessly in tune with their true self.

Small children are guided by nature and thus are still aligned to the source of their desires, their joy and their light. This, I believe, is the reason why they shine so brightly. It is also why we delight in being in their presence. If we are conscious enough to allow ourselves into their magic world and spend time with them, we automatically tune in to the frequency of creativity and joy.

118

*Every child is born
imaginative and playful.
Being creative is your
natural state of being.
No learning required.*

This frequency of love – so naturally allowed by us when we are children – is an abundant source radiating far beyond our beating heart. Yet as we enter adulthood, we have conformed to society and adapted ourselves out of alignment with it. As we gain knowledge about how the reality into which we are born works, we gradually lose our instant and pure connection to this source, containing all our desires, curiosity and imagination.

By conforming to society – in order to function, be 'normal' and 'fit in' – we suppress our innate spontaneity. Being spontaneous requires us to be present in the NOW, but we worry too much about the future and dwell too often on the past.

119

*Children are so busy
being in the present,
they have no time
to worry about the future
or dwell on the past.*

How to repress this vibrant spontaneity is something we learn early on, from the grown-ups around us.

There are people who say that wisdom is the product of a learning process through a well-lived life and through contemplation. And surely that is a part of the truth. But being wise is not only something you *learn intellectually* by the passing of time – it is also something you can *experience viscerally* any time.

120 | *Being wise is something we all are*
when our mind is crystal clear
and our heart is wide open.

Children are among the wisest beings on Earth and yet they do not have much life experience. Instead, their wisdom lies in their understanding and appropriation of the concept of time. To children, time simply does not exist. You either 'do stuff' or you don't. When you 'do stuff' you move, when you 'don't do stuff' you are still. That's it.

Well, that is pretty much a description of the fundamental principle of creation – All That Is (stillness) manifests itself into physical reality (movement). Your source is a creative creator. Align with your source from within.

121 | *Conformity kills creativity.*
Stay curious. Ask questions.
Be yourself. Stand courageous!
Play! Enjoy! Laugh more.

122 | *The only truly free humans*
are the children
because they have not
forgotten the art
of playing and daydreaming.

YOU are creative

123 | We are ALL born curious and creative.
| EVERYTHING else is conditioned behaviour.

One question I am often asked is 'How can we learn to be more creative?' The answer is as simple as the actions we need to take in order to become more creative.

To begin with, it is not a question of *learning* how to be creative. It is more a question of how we can *play* with ideas and *allow* ourselves to have *fun* in the process. Every single child is born playful and creative, so being imaginative is our natural state of mind; consequently we do not need to *learn* something we already *know* how to do.

One of the major 'brick walls' that block our creativity is fear of doing 'the wrong thing' or 'making a fool of ourselves'. So, if we want to make full use of our innate creativity, we have to start trusting each other in the creative process and cultivate a zesty feeling of playful inventiveness. In an environment that allows us to make 'mistakes' and learn from them, *anyone* can be creative. What we have to do is:

Remember how to play.

124 | *EXPECT joy and fun.*
KNOW that things will work out for the best.
GO with your flow

Remember how to boost your creativity.

125 | *RECALL the feeling of unlimited possibilities.*
TRUST your self, and above all, be yourself.
PLAY more. Enjoy more.

Remember how to reach your highest frequency of creativity.

126 | *Be intensely yourself.*
Do not compare yourself with others.
Don't do it just for the success,
do it for the JOY of it!

All new things 'enter' reality through a creative mind.

127 | *Imagination is*
a tool of creation.

Imagine,
dream,
wish,
play!

Creativity equals courage

128 | *The brave dare to go*
where no one else has been.
Be courageous: dare to explore
what is hidden within.

Creativity means allowing your imagination to bring something new and never-before-seen into being. When we are not willing to go beyond our creative comfort zone with its existing limitations, nothing new can be created. From that point of view, creativity and courage are intimately entwined.

In fact, there can be no creativity without courage because expressing your self creatively requires the bravery to go beyond the conforming boundaries of conventional beliefs, ideas and voices.

129 | *It takes courage:*
to have trust in your own ideas,
to stay true to your self,
to dare to explore,
to play and make 'mistakes'.

And it takes courage to go against subconscious 'herd-behaviour' and to consciously express your individuality and uniqueness – even at the risk of being excluded from the group. Consider the alternative: conforming means giving up a part of your true self, which is always unique, always different than anyone else and always unparalleled to anything. Without exception. Is it not worth exploring that unique part of who you are? Even at the cost of doing it in solitude?

The way I see it, conformism (or 'sheepism') is one of the most harmful forms of ignorance. Not only does it affect those who succumb to it, it also affects the entire human race on a core level of reality. Without the creative brave ones who consistently challenge the status quo, we would never expand as a species, or grow and experience anything new.

Conformism might seem like a private matter, but in fact it creates 'space' for low and negative energies – such as inertia, 'short-sightedness', ignorance and emotional numbness – to manifest as 'solid' reality in the form of circumstances, relationships, obstacles, problems and violence: affecting *everyone* standing in its frequency.

Think about this:

130 | *Every time you conform to something because the majority thinks it is 'the right thing', you stop yourself from exploring who YOU truly are.*

You deny yourself the opportunity to appreciate your true identity, your deepest desires and your life purpose. You miss a chance to be creative and to grow in your consciousness –

which, by the way, is the reason why you and every living soul on this planet came here in the first place.

131

Stay brave.
Ask questions.
Be creative.

Part 7

Why Now Is Your Point of Power

NOW and the illusion of time

132 | *There is no past or future,*
unless you THINK it.

YOU are the creator
of your past and future.
Your point of creation is NOW.

We are born into a reality in which the 'boundaries' between past, future and now seem to be rigidly fixed. Consequently, time is considered to be strictly linear, absolutely accurate and perceived as the same thing by each and every one of us. We are conditioned to 'see' our past as a determinant, crucial and unchanging part of who we are now.

In our society, it seems to be more important what we were doing in the past than what we are actually doing in the now. In fact, our entire identity as a civilization is based on this seemingly fixed and static concept of the past. As human beings we are considered to be the sum total of all our memories and experiences. Which, by the way, are supposed to reside in an inaccessible and unchanging past, out of our reach.

Since we take it for granted that 'you can't change the past', we simply see no other option than to 'drag it along' with us into the future, thus solidly rooting all our present

NOW-moments into the status quo of our past or into the uncertainty of our future.

This creates the necessary illusion of linear time and continuity, but it also locks us into a belief that the future *depends* on the past. The way I see it, nothing can be further from the truth. The concept of time is much more flexible than we are taught to believe. The future and the past do not exist per se: they are just anticipations and memories perceived in the eternal NOW. It is just 'noise' from the past and 'static' from the future, created in our mind when we choose to think about it in the NOW.

133 | *The past gives you an illusion of identity.*
Seemingly solid, it predicts a future you.
But the real YOU can only exist in the NOW.

Actually, NOW is the only place in time and space where YOU are. Your consciousness expands beyond the physical expression of YOU and beyond time, space and matter. 'Events' like your memories seem to reside 'outside' physical reality, so in order for you to 'recollect' them, you need to 'go' into your expanded consciousness to 'recall' the information and 'recreate' it in your mind.

Everything occupying your mind is a creation existing *only* because you choose to *think of it* in the NOW – even your memories and your thoughts about the future. The way I see it, a memory is a very flexible concept of time and space and it can be used as a powerful tool in the NOW to create a more joyous future. We will be exploring memories more in the next chapters.

134 | *Spend less time in*
'I was' and 'I will be'.
The only 'place' where
you can make a change
is in the 'I AM'.

It does not matter what you did in the past or what you want to do in the future. All that matters is what you are doing NOW. Some of you might say, 'What if I did something bad in my past? Aren't there any consequences?' Of course there are, but seeking forgiveness or forgiving yourself in the NOW will always alter the way you look at the past and thus change the future.

The past only exists as a memory in your mind. It is altered and reshaped by your feelings each time you recall it in the NOW. If you look at yourself in your memory from a slightly different angle, you might see new facets of yourself, thus changing the 'colour' of the entire experience.

135 | *People from your past*
obscuring your heart
are nothing more than
shadows in your mind.

There are no shadows
in the light.

Dwelling on obstacles in your past will not bring the future you want. Looking at the past and changing your way of interpreting it in the NOW, will.

136 | *You are creating your...*
... PRESENT with what you BELIEVE,
... PAST with what you REMEMBER,
... FUTURE with what you IMAGINE.

YOU are the one choosing your truths. YOU are the one re-creating your memories. YOU are the one playing with your imagination.

137 | *Without YOU, there is*
no PAST,
no PRESENT
and no FUTURE.

NOW is your access point to everything.

Memories

138 | *The only thing in life*
you cannot control
is being born and dying.
Everything in between
is at your disposal
to shape, change and enjoy.

We are truly powerful beings. Everything that happens between our first and our last breath is within our power to transform, change and mould in a beneficial way.

What happened to you in your past, when you were a child, is not your responsibility. It is what you are doing with those experiences – those memories – in the NOW that is your responsibility. If your memories are holding you in a victimized state, it is your job to change that.

Memories are not as static as you might believe. They are simply energy that you 'carry' with you, containing facts with emotions attached to them. While you cannot change the actual facts in your memories – for example, the age you were at the time, where you were and with whom – you *can* change the *feelings* attached to the facts.

We have memories for a reason – there is a purpose to remembering our past. Everything that is in our lives now is there for a reason. We are not born with the ability to remember things just because our reality works that way. There is more to it than that.

The way I see it, if we live in an unconditionally loving Universe, there must be a *beneficial* reason for us to remember the past and to store the memories. No matter what kind of memories we are hiding deep in our hearts, we are supposed to *use* them in order to evolve, in order to expand and in order to unfold who we are.

You can choose to experience your memories from a more advantageous perspective. For instance, since there is no single interpretation of a memory, you can explore a bad childhood memory from a perspective of strength in the NOW, instead of from a perspective of victimhood from the past.

Nothing is written in stone. Everything is constantly moving, in constant creation.

139 | *Your memories become REAL only because you CHOOSE to 'experience' them again in the PRESENT.*

There is a beneficial way of looking at FEAR. There is a beneficial way of looking at ENVY. There is a beneficial way of looking at HATE. These negative feelings are a contrast to who you truly are.

140 | *By looking at what you are not,*
you can better define what you are.

So a memory, even if it is a bad one, is there for you to use in a good and helpful way. It allows you to see your own strengths in a past of weaknesses and vulnerability.

141 | *Beneath the surface of weakness and sorrow,*
true strength and joy are always present.
It is the divine yin and yang law of nature.

Change your past

142 | *It does not matter who you WERE.*
All that really matters is who you ARE.

We are the creators of time and space – we literally think them into existence. This is so because without an observer, there can be no past, no present and no future. Where is the past stored and where does the future come from? Since the past only exists in our memory and the future is created in our imagination, the answer must be, *our mind*.

We tend to perceive the present as a result of the past because there is a 'built-in' illusion of linear continuity in our reality-experience. We think that the past is unchangeable or 'written in stone' and that the future is unpredictable and etheric – totally out of our control. Thus we walk around in the present feeling guilt about the past, while at the same time feeling anxious about the future.

If you think about it, it really does not matter what you have done in the past or what you plan to do in the future. All that really matters is what you are doing in the NOW. Because NOW is the only 'time' that exists.

Every 'NOW-moment' is an opportunity to change not only your future, but also your past. You might not be aware of this, but you can use memories of your past as effective 'adjustment tools' in the present. By changing the way you interpret the information stored in your memory, you can alter your perception of yourself: now and in your future.

Let me give you an example. A long time ago in a remote memory of mine, I am a five-year-old girl. Insignificant to my father and unwanted by my mother, I am silently aware of my 'outsiderness'. One day it was decided that the family would go on a day trip to a cave nearby. I remember feeling very exited, but as it turned out, my mother concluded that 'there wasn't enough room for me' in the car, and I should stay with my aunt.

I remember thinking as I watched everyone take a seat in the car, *But I'm not big – there must be room for me... somewhere.* When my family had left, I sat down by the roadside with my aunt. And I made up my mind, right there and then, that I was going to see the cave anyway.

So I started putting pebbles and stones together, one on top of the other, forming them into a very small, hollow mould. When I was done, I turned to my aunt and said, 'Let's go in!'

To others, this might seem like an insignificant incident, but to me it was a fractal of a pattern in my childhood. It was an uncomfortable and sad memory that reminded me of constantly being set aside by my mother. And it was profound because it defined me in my present as unloved, unwanted and unworthy.

But when I made a choice in the present to look at the memory from a different angle as a mature spectator – actively focusing on finding a positive aspect in the memory – what I saw was not a pitiable, unwanted little girl but a playful, strong and determined soul. The 'present' in the present for me was that I stopped perceiving myself as a victim and chose to see that this creative and smart being is who I really was and always have been.

Every memory comes with an emotion imbedded within it. When you twist the perspective from which you experience your memory, it gives you a slightly altered but equally true memory that can be beneficial for the construction of your future. The 'facts' stay the same – you just extract a new feeling from the memory.

143 | *Everything has a darker and a brighter side. What you see depends on your PERSPECTIVE.*

Look at your memory from a different perspective and the feeling changes – the present changes the past and affects the future. With the retrieved and updated information from your 'old' memories, you can recreate yourself into the 'YOU' you want to become and manifest a reality of your choice.

Contemplate this:

144 | *The past is recreated in the present every time you revisit a memory.*

Your past cannot affect your future, unless YOU let it do so.

You give your past and your memories meaning. They are yours to play with and explore. Since the present is *not* an automatic result of a 'fixed' past, you can freely decide what is useful for you in your memories and what is not.

Find the good stuff, keep it and let go of the rest.

145

Every new NOW-moment is full of opportunities and possibilities to recreate yourself.

Be in the present.
It is the only moment
in which anything –
new or old –
can be created.

All you have to do is see the 'presents' in the present.

Set your intention

146 | *Today I will feel at ease with myself and enjoy my being.*

One morning I woke up in a most unusual way. Even though my eyes were closed and my body was still in a very relaxed state of being, I felt fully awake. There was a surreal clarity in my thoughts as I heard my own inner voice softly ask: 'What is your intention today?' What happened next can best be described as the scene from the movie *Bruce Almighty* where Bruce and God have a conversation on how to say a prayer properly.

Automatically, my mind started going through the things I needed *to do* that day. I answered: 'I have to pick up my clothes at the dry cleaners. I need to go to the bank. I have to call my dentist. I have to talk to my publisher...' and on and on it went. Suddenly, I was interrupted abruptly by my inner voice saying loudly: 'STOP! I did not ask for your schedule... I asked: WHAT IS YOUR INTENTION TODAY?'

...What is your intention today?... I made a full stop in my thoughts and without opening my eyes, I just slowly breathed in and out.

147 | *This is a new day.*
It has not yet begun.
It will never return.
It is a unique day.
One of a kind.
Treasure it.

My inner voice explained to me: 'You are the imaginer, creator, explorer and consumer of this day. What kind of emotions and experiences do you want to fill it with? What is your intention?'

I thought, *Oh, it is not about the things I need* to do *but the experiences I want to explore...* I get it... And I answered: 'I want to be fully aware, every single NOW-moment of the day. I want to be able to give and receive love in every encounter I have during today. I want to enjoy my being.'

Immediately, my inner voice affirmed that I was on the right track by saying: 'Now we are talking. That is a clear intention. Everything else is just noise. Now, seize the day! Do not let it slip away. Go and explore!'

When you establish a clear intention for a day, it works like a filter through which you 'look' at everything you experience. You still do the things you need to do, only you perceive them differently. Set your intention! Here are some suggestions for clear intentions:

148 | *Today I will allow love,*
creativity and joy
to flow freely through me.

149 | *Today I will make a fresh start by releasing all fear, guilt and doubt.*

150 | *Today I will consciously choose to stay out of drama, negativity and energy-draining people.*

I am

151

I am a curious, playful spirit exploring the polarity of the LIGHT and DARKNESS in my reality.

My HEART is the place in time and space where SOUL and MATTER unite.

My BRAIN is the place in time and space where SPIRIT and MIND unite.

My 'GUT' is the place in time and space where INTUITION and EMOTION unite.

My BREATH is the place in time and space where I and the UNIVERSE unite.

I AM the NOW where ALL becomes ONE.

Part 8

Why God = You

What is GOD?

152 | *GOD is in the shades and light on a canvas,*
manifested through a connection between
an artist's sensitive eye and tender touch.

GOD is in the perfect combination of tone
and scale expressed through the creative
mind and talented body of a musician
or a dancer.

GOD is in the 'ink' of a writer's words,
suddenly appearing in perfect order
and rhythm on a blank piece of paper.

GOD is the invisible FORCE
that holds everything together
in perfect geometric harmony
on a quantum level of existence.

In the Spiritual World,
GOD is the ESSENCE
of every-thing and no-thing.

In My Reality, GOD is in the LOVE I feel
for my son and my husband
and in my GRATITUDE
for BEING able to share my thoughts.

Who are YOU?

We are ONE consciousness experiencing itself through a multitude of singularity points of awareness. Every ONE is unique, yet we are ONE.

If the word 'God' does not resonate with you, feel free to change it to whatever is the right frequency for you. Here are some suggestions: the Source, All That Is, the Force, the Universe.

153

You cannot SEE God, because God is the SEER in you.

You cannot HEAR God, because God is the LISTENER in you.

You cannot SPEAK to God, because God is the THINKER in you.

Know this: you are a perfect fractal of All That Is. Your source works through you, not outside of you. YOU are the creator of everything in your reality. In that sense, YOU can never be 'lost', because your life and everything in it is YOUR creation.

154

Who are YOU?
YOU are God. GOD is you.
You are the ONE. The ONE is YOU.

Dying Gods and Goddesses

155 | *Everything in the Universe is made of infinite energy, including you and me.*

Energy cannot be destroyed, only transformed.

We are eternal souls 'pretending' to be mortal humans – just to explore the contrast between life and death and to heighten the experience and appreciation of living by undoubtedly 'believing' we can die...

We are light beings. Quantum physics suggests that all matter, including the human body, is made of waves of light. In that sense, we are pure energy. And energy cannot be destroyed. It can only change form. Our origin is infinite, eternal and divine. Reality is just a stage in the Theatre of Life, where we act out the role of a 'dying' God or Goddess, just for the joy of being 'alive'.

156 | *To believe we can lose something, heightens the experience of having it.*

Take time to appreciate life, even in the smallest of things.

Why knowing who YOU are matters

157

*The more you realize who YOU truly are,
the less you seek approval.*

*The more you know and respect yourself,
the less you fear rejection,
setbacks and 'failure'.*

*The more inner power you gain,
the less outer control you allow.*

*The more you are your true self,
the more you inspire others
to be their true selves.*

*The more you know who YOU truly are,
the more you accept and appreciate
what OTHERS are.*

*Every ONE is unique.
We are all ONE.*

YOU in relation to others

158 | *The whole point of relationships is to experience a different perspective on reality and thus expand in your consciousness.*

Relationships exist so we can experience perspectives other than our own and through that, grow in awareness and understanding. Every time you try to change someone's perspective – to make it become the *same* as your own – you miss the point of the connection. That is why people in a relationship sometimes drift apart. They miss the *point* of the connection...

The differences between us are not obstacles to overcome, but opportunities to 'take in' more of our reality, because joined perspectives offer a bigger 'piece of the cake'. The whole point of a relationship is to *expand* your knowledge about your reality and your self.

A relationship is like a mirror that shows you images of who you are in that particular setting. It reflects a facet of your self from a slightly different perspective than your own. In other words, it shows you more of who *you* are. If you do not like the image reflected back at you, you need to make a change from within.

159 | *Forgive and communicate,*
or leave.

Part 9

Why You = Love

YOU are LOVE

160 | *We live in a world of magic.*
Thoughts turn into matter,
infinity unfolds as space
and eternity flows into time
while you read these words.

When I was a child I could 'see' the enchanted 'machinery' behind the real world. I knew that the Universe and I were one and that the Universe was my partner in creation. All I had to do was ask and the Universe would provide. Unconditionally.

Since I chose to be born to parents who, due to their own emotionally scarce childhoods, did not know how to express genuine love, my inner conversations with the Universe were often about love: 'What is love?' I would ask. 'Where does love come from?' and 'How can I get more of it?'

Sometimes, when meeting a friendly stray cat on the street or cuddling my teddy bear in bed, I could sense the funny paradox of love. You know, the one where 'the more you give, the more you have'. But I also knew all too well, through emotionally painful experience, that 'you cannot give what you do not have'.

During my countless silent conversations with the Universe I have come to understand that love is ONE with no equals.

Nothing else in our reality has the same 'properties' as love. There is a peculiar difference between love and all negative, dark emotions such as fear or hate. Not just the obvious difference, but a deeper, more profound one.

I have always been fascinated by a line of dialogue from the 1990 movie *Ghost* that I think describes the true nature of our source; but also why love is sacred and everything else is secondary. As Sam, one of the main characters, is passing away, his spirit turns to his beloved and says:

'It's amazing, Molly. The love inside, you take it with you.'

What he is saying in the moment of physical death is that all you truly 'own' is your self. Everything else is 'borrowed' in the reality of time and space. And since your core is unconditional love, then love is all you can 'take with you' when you return to your source.

In that sense:

161 | *Love is all that is real and everything else is just a persistent illusion in time and space.*

Let me put it another way:

162 | *No infant knows how to hate. That is something we learn as we grow up.*

Genuine love is unconditional, whereas negative emotions such as hate require specific conditions to exist. Hate must be preceded by an action or a thought. One thought follows another thought, creating the notion of time, which means that hate needs time to exist. And since hate is an excluding frequency – meaning it separates and 'pushes' things away – it also needs space.

So, beyond the 'reality' of time and space there is no 'situation' and no 'room' for hate to dwell in. Love on the other hand is instant, all-embracing and all-inclusive. It does not have to be preceded by anything. It simply is. Always available in the NOW. For the joy of being.

Love is the base ingredient in the fabric of the Universe, working with infinite precision and patience. Like mathematics and geometry, love is a universal 'language' understood by all of us. The saying goes that 'love is blind', but the way I see it, love is not blind: it is just a higher frequency transforming everything when felt in that vibration.

163 | *Love not only transforms you from within, it transforms everything you focus your mind on from without.*

Love creates an atmosphere where even the 'darkness' is included, allowed and transformed within its warm, compassionate light. You are connecting to pure love and truth because that is what your source is 'made of'. That is the essence of who you truly are. When you are aligned to that source, no thought can be based in fear or hate because you know love from its purest form – your self. You are the infinite source of love.

Your free will to always choose love is a treasure, giving you endless opportunities to transform everything you focus your attention on. Choose love and see the magic behind the real world.

Because you see:

164 | *The Universe is always listening...*
... and providing.
Unconditionally!

YOU are the shining ONE

'Shine on you crazy diamond'
PINK FLOYD

You were perfect long before you were born. And when taking your first deep breath of life, you were a flawless, beautiful being, lacking nothing. We all were. Every single one of us. Without exception.

We begin this physical life as luminous, curious, joy-seeking children, fragile yet intriguingly fearless, naïve yet intuitively wise, dependent yet totally trusting. With the passing of time, our inner pureness slowly wears down, while we become painfully confronted by the limitations and scarcity manifested by the grown-up 'outer' world.

Holding my newborn son for the first time, I realized how wise and beautiful we are when we enter this reality. But this fundamental authenticity is conditioned away by the society and culture in which we live, and as we grow up, we forget our inherent validity.

In order to 'fit in', we intuitively retract our shining core and hide it from harm, somewhere deep in the secret chambers of our heart. We quickly learn how to use masks, disguises and 'tricks' in order to be seen, heard and acknowledged by others. And by the time we enter adulthood we have become masters at hiding our inner shining being – by repressing and ignoring it while compulsively conforming our selves to 'normal' and to 'others'.

The society we grow up in conditions us to feel inadequate and not good enough, and we often think, *If only I learn this, or do that, I will have a true value.*

We focus so much on improvement and on getting better at the wrong things, that we gradually pull a veil of forgetfulness tighter and tighter around the incredible divine and inherent power we have within us. And before we know it, we have completely forgotten who we truly are. We have adapted; we have become normal, and boringly average.

I remember as a child being confused when people asked me what I wanted to 'be' when I grew up. Why couldn't I just be myself? Why would I need to become something other than what I already was? The way I saw it, the grown-ups were implying that being your self is not enough and that you need to change the ONE you are NOW in order to become some-one in the future. It did not make sense to me.

165 | *Never lose yourself in the jungles of the 'grown-up' world.*
Explore YOUR truths.
TRUST what you find.

As a child I loved drawing, so I thought about becoming a drawing teacher. I loved reading, so I tried to find occupations that would put me in rooms with lots of books – like working as a librarian, or being a scientist at a university.

I did not like injustice, so I would fight the bullies in school when they teased younger children in the schoolyard. And when I look back at all this, I see a pattern. I am not a drawing teacher, but I got a master's degree in art history. I did not become a librarian, but I write books. And I still fight injustice: not with my fists, as I did as a child, but with my words and thoughts.

So you see, everything always works out the way it is supposed to, as long as you stay true to yourself and who you are.

166

A child does not spend its time wondering 'Who am I?' – because it KNOWS.

It simply uses the time to play, imagine and enjoy its being in the NOW.

Considering how magnificent you were when you were born and considering that you cannot be less than that now, then being who you truly are is only a question of recognizing your divine self and remembering who you truly are.

You are the ground in which your soul has taken root to explore the lightness of itself. The *only* limitation is your imagination.

167 | *The only way to find your divine self*
is by relentlessly BEING yourself.

You are unique.
There is no one like you!
You are... ONE... of a kind.

Exploring this does not have to be hard work. It does not have to take any time or space. No yoga mat required, no mentor needed, no herbs infused. All you need is YOU. Just be still and see the *beauty* in the tiniest things; recognize *love* in the smallest acts and you will automatically align your self with the divine YOU – the shining YOU.

When you align your personality with your soul, your true self will find a way to shine through in every thought you have and in every action you take. Do not wear a mask. Do not hide. Do not pretend. Because in the end, being YOU is what you came here to do. So lighten up and be delighted! Illuminate yourself and shine!

168 | *Shortcuts to finding your true self:*
ALWAYS follow your PASSION.
Do what you LOVE.
TRUST your SELF.
ENJOY the process!

Perfect imperfections

Many of us walk this Earth with a persistent feeling of being incomplete. It is almost as if we are lacking a vital part that is responsible for our happiness and wellbeing. If we could find this missing piece, then and only then, could we be happy and the 'puzzle' would be complete; then and only then, would we feel accomplished and fulfilled; then and only then, would we feel the joy of who we truly are.

So we keep on looking and looking. Lifetime after lifetime. Never, not even for a single second, do we stop and consider this: what if this 'lack' we have been conditioned to define as a defect and shortage in ourselves, is actually an advantage and an essential part of being in a human body?

What if this 'incompleteness' actually is just an 'opening' in something that is initially perfectly complete? What if this opening, this 'crack' in our perception of our selves, actually is an opportunity – a chance given to us so we can stay open to new experiences and learn more?

I mean, if you were complete, whole, full, closed, finished and done, then what would be the purpose of exploring this physical life? Why would you be here?

169 | *You are not here to suffer from being 'imperfect' and 'incomplete'.*

You are here to enjoy all your perfect imperfections.

You are here to expand All That Is with your explorations in time and space. So, consider being incomplete good for you. It means that you are *open* to change and *open* to new experiences. You are under constant construction. We all are. Embrace it.

The 13th-century Persian poet and Sufi mystic Rumi reminds us of this innate imperfection of all things. He writes: 'The wound is the place where Light enters' – playing with the thought that every thing has a scar or a crack in it, allowing the light to illuminate us from within.

170 | *Being 'perfect' is actually being who you are.*

*Completely,
fully,
utterly
and unconditionally
YOU.*

YOU are your biggest asset

Most of us go through life without acknowledging or even realizing the dormant potential residing within each and every one of us. We waste our talent and inner resources by working hard on things that are not important to us and by conforming to belief systems that are not created by us.

We allow others to dictate what is or isn't true in our reality, and in the process of conforming into 'normal', we forget who we are. We repress the outstanding potential we inherently host within our being. Simply put, we throw away our biggest assets in order to be accepted by others and feel that we belong somewhere.

171

'Lazy' is a label
designed to make you feel guilty
when you avoid doing
what OTHERS expect of you.

Never let others
define YOU.

Be your own definer.

Trying to be 'normal' by doing things you do not enjoy, but feel you *have* to do, only makes you feel 'straightjacketed' and powerless. By now, you probably know that you literally vibrate inertia and procrastination into existence when you ignore your self and your passions. To change frequency and free yourself from stagnation, you have to start doing what *you* LOVE now – otherwise your true skills and talents will stay in your future for ever.

172 | *YOU are your biggest asset.*
Start exploring who YOU are,
what YOU want
and where YOU are heading.

This is a really serious business. If you do not know *who* you are, how will you know *what* you want? If you do not know *what* you want, how will you know when you have *received* it? So you see, knowing your self is essential for your entire *being*.

To get a clear 'sound' of who YOU are, stop reacting to 'outer' noise and start listening to your own 'inner' silence. You do not need to think, say or do anything. Just relax. Your access to that inner sound and power is always there. Patiently waiting for YOU.

Just take time to be still and you will automatically enter your infinite resources, your own 'power zone'. One of the best and easiest ways to explore your power zone is through creative imagination. Visualization and daydreaming come as free 'tools' from a never-ending source – YOU.

173 | *Imagine in detail how*
your reality would look,
feel and be if everything
you wish for became real.

Start daydreaming about the things you LOVE in your life. Send pictures to your brain of what you enjoy doing, of things that excite you and of who you want to become. Allow yourself to *feel* the joy of *having* everything you desire, of *being* everything you desire and of *doing* everything you desire. Stay in that frequency for as long as you enjoy doing it. Do it as often as you feel like it.

174 | *You create your own reality by what you believe about it.*

Use your imagination to mould, sculpt and paint an image of who YOU believe you are.

When you daydream you imagine your own creation by making an image in the present of who you are in the future. In a daydream you can persistently explore who you are and what you want in your reality. So imagine yourself being the best you in every NOW-moment and you will effortlessly change your image, frame by frame.

Use your inner resources to change your outer reality. I cannot write that loud enough: USE YOUR INNER RESOURCES TO CHANGE YOUR OUTER REALITY!

YOU are your biggest asset; thus exploring who YOU are is fundamental. You are a magnificent soul, full of divine potential. Everything else is conditioned illusion. The *only* limitation is your imagination.

175

Lighten up! Play!
Ask questions.
Enjoy being you!

After all,
being YOU is what you
came here to do.

It's as simple as that!

Part 10

Why You Are the Point of Creative Manifestation

YOU are the Imaginer

176 | *How conscious of*
who YOU truly are,
are you?

Explore your beliefs.
They contain your 'reality'.

What if your life – as you imagine it – was limited by fictional boundaries in your mind, blocking you from truly becoming the best you?

What if everything you think, imagine and believe to be true about yourself and your reality turned out to be borrowed, copied or repeated information – acquired and accepted subconsciously over time, by you?

What if you, unknowingly, have assembled bits of beliefs here and there on your journey through life, accepting them at face value because they were presented to you by people whom you, at the time, considered trustworthy and reliable? Knowing this, would you be willing to challenge your beliefs and change the image of YOU?

All your beliefs about yourself and your self-worth reside in your subconscious mind. Your subconscious mind contains the things you think about yourself when you are alone and the things you believe and 'know' about who you imagine you are.

Most of your responses, attitudes and behaviours were 'preprogrammed' in your early childhood by the culture into which you were born. As a rule, people tend to mirror the programmes presented to them unconditionally and automatically – just to blend in, and to avoid the fear and pain of being different and alone.

177 | *You are manifesting your reality 24/7.*

You are 'on' all the time.

How much of this time are you conscious of what you are creating?

Honestly speaking, most of us have no idea that we are manifesting *everything* in our reality, *all the time*. We seem to be 'cruising' through this reality on autopilot. Why is that so? Because the reality you are manifesting or generating is very much determined by what you habitually 'know' and *automatically* believe about your reality.

Most of your core beliefs about yourself and your reality are obscured by a veil of unconsciousness. This is because you allowed them, unconditionally, into your mind during your early childhood. You did this by mirroring your parents, siblings and neighbours – long before you could speak and 'translate' the beliefs into conscious words and concepts.

School, the media, news, books and movies affected your way of thinking in your past and solidified the 'preprogrammed' beliefs about how reality works. All of which literally makes your present life someone else's creation. Because if the reality you are generating is based on unconscious, automatic responses that were created in your past, then your reality NOW (the reflection you are looking at in the present) is not your own creation: it is generated through you, but not BY you.

And this is where most people get stuck. They keep focusing on the reflection they are generating in the now, not realizing that it is a mirror. Or more accurately, a result of a frequency – a vibratory state of mind – from the past.

This is how reality becomes a loop in time and space in which unconscious beliefs are perpetuated by the past, creating a future you do not want because it is not based on who YOU truly are in the NOW. This is also how recurring obstacles and situations become a deceptively 'normal' part of your everyday reality.

178 | *To make a change you need to stop staring at the reflection and start taking care of the frequency behind the belief that created it in the first place.*

There are two things YOU need to do before you can start allowing your reality to change in the direction YOU desire:

- Understand and acknowledge your part in the creation of your own reality.

- Take full responsibility for it.

Let's start by understanding and acknowledging your part.

179

What you believe,
you perceive.

You are the definer
of your reality-experience.

Since you are the one creating your own reality-experience, your beliefs are only as flexible as *you* are. The more willing you are to 'play' with your reality, the easier it becomes for you to create from a desire-based perspective. When you start asking questions like *Why? Is it really so? How come...? What if...?* about the most basic things in your life, and you start trusting your inner answers, magic happens. There are no 'stupid' questions. Every belief is challengeable and more importantly, changeable. The essential thing is to start redefining your reality by reimagining it!

180

Your life is shaped
in the image of YOU,
and you are the Imaginer.

Everything you encounter in your life had its beginnings in the connection between your unique mind and the quantum field (All That Is, Source, the Universe, God). Events, things and situations always have their beginnings in the non-physical realm of reality. They exist as neutral 'containers' in the field of your frequency.

Try to imagine the quantum field as a big 'toy box' and yourself as the one choosing which 'toys' you want to play with. Your emotions set the tone of your experience. The situation (or event or thing) 'hangs around' in the quantum field 'toy box', waiting for you to notice it. The moment you 'see' the situation, you have attracted your chosen 'toy' to you. You 'look' at the 'toy' through your unique focus-point of consciousness and fill it with what to you seems like appropriate content.

For instance, you might see a glass as half full, your neighbour might say it is half empty while your best friend might wonder what the difference is, since the glass can always be refilled. It is the same 'container' but with totally different 'content'.

181

There is something for you to learn from every situation, happening and relationship in your reality.

You are 'picking' the situation out of the 'toy box'. Of all the potentiality in the quantum field, you are choosing to manifest the specific one on which you are focusing your awareness. It is your definition of the manifested situations, things and events that gives them meaning, sense and significance. They have no meaning until you 'own' them.

In the physical world it might appear as if these situations had an in-built meaning – because they seem to be exterior and affect you from the 'outside'. But when you grasp that you create your own reality, by being the one picking out the 'toys' with your frequency, you will also understand that reality is created from the inside-out.

This means that the situation does not come with a pre-attached meaning. Instead, it is created *after* you give off a vibration of certain emotions and beliefs. Your frequency can be likened to a 'play-mood' – the one you are in helps you 'find' the appropriate 'toy' out of all the infinite ones in the quantum field. Happy 'play-mood' attracts 'bright toys'. Sad 'play-mood' attracts 'dull toys'... and so on.

Do you see how important your thoughts, feelings and beliefs are? If you understand this basic pattern, you can use it to figure out *why* you are attracting certain situations in your life and *what* you are choosing to perceive in them.

182 | *It is your beliefs that create the situations, not the other way around.*

The key is to realize that the situation is originally neutral. This is a bit tricky, but the truth is that it is like a blank sheet of paper on which you inscribe your meaning. You are the creator of the situation (you are picking it out), the observer (you are 'looking' at it), and the consumer (you are experiencing it).

Your interpretation of your creation is a projection of YOU, and therefore it contains whatever you consciously or subconsciously 'choose' to fill it with. Your belief systems provide you with the 'filling material' in abundance.

When you understand that the situation comes without a specific pre-attached meaning, you can start looking at the events in your life as perfect opportunities to get to know yourself better and to gain more control over what you attract into your reality.

This is valuable information because it gives you chances to explore specific beliefs and to change them if they do not please you. When you change your 'play-mood', you pick up other 'toys' and therefore the game changes.

183 | *Change the belief and your reality changes accordingly.*

This leads us to the second thing YOU have to incorporate into your system of beliefs before you can start allowing your reality to move in the direction YOU desire. You need to take full responsibility for everything in your life.

184 | *Life does not happen TO you. It happens THROUGH you.*

Your frequency determines the sound, taste, look and feel of your Universe.

With this in mind you will understand that you cannot change your reality if you think someone else is responsible for it. Life is not made up of random events that cluelessly pop up here and there. Your life is *your* creation, perfectly mirroring *your* frequency.

So, instead of externalizing your power by asking 'Why is this happening to me?', take back your power and accept full responsibility. Ask yourself, 'Why am I choosing to experience this in a specific way?' and 'What can I learn about myself and my reality through this experience?'

Answering these questions will help you shift your frequency and thus change your future. It is very important that you apply all the information and knowledge you gain in a productive and positive way, without the heaviness of guilt, blame and failure.

185

When reality presents you with low-frequency situations, relationships, events and things, it is actually reminding you that you need to heighten your frequency.

It is a reminder that it is time to start redefining your beliefs and reimagining your self again. What your reality is telling you is that you need to take care of your frequency by embracing your desires, passions, dreams and wishes. How you *feel* is important because emotions affect your frequency and your frequency determines your reality.

Ignoring negativity and focusing on the brighter side of everything you encounter, and deliberately staying in a positive state of mind by persistently imagining yourself in a future you desire, is neither selfish nor naïve. It is about managing your state of being and about becoming a more deliberate creator by using your imagination as it is meant to be used: to imagine a bright future into existence.

186

*Ignoring negativity
is not about being selfish.*

*It is about taking care of
YOUR frequency
and the energy YOU
allow into the world
through YOU.*

Ignoring negativity, then, is actually a way of taking responsibility for what YOU choose to create.

Obstacles

Your reality is what you believe it to be. Let's say that you fear what the future holds for you. When you tune your frequency to fear, all you can perceive is fear. Everything contradicting the state of fear becomes invisible to you, because you have chosen to focus your awareness and beliefs on the frequency of fear. And the Universe responds unconditionally to that frequency by providing you with the requested 'correct' information.

187 | *What you focus your mind on grows.*
Where your attention goes, energy flows.

It is like listening to the radio. All the other stations are there, but you can only hear the one you have *chosen* to listen to. That is why you have to *consciously* change your emotional frequency to a different one – one that is beneficial to you – by changing the direction of your thoughts.

Here is an esoteric truth that can change the way you perceive your own power. Since we live in a dualistic reality in which every problem and obstacle has a darker and a brighter side, you *always* have a *choice*. You cannot remove the problem or obstacle, but you have been granted the gift of free will to choose which side of it you want to focus your attention on – which side you wish to feed with your energy.

In other words, you are the ONE deciding *how* a problem or obstacle affects you. You can choose to give away your innate power and dwell on the problem for months and years, ruining your life with it. Or you can choose to use your innate power and realize that you are *bigger* than the problem and grow from it. Viewed from a higher perspective, obstacles are not in your reality to make your life miserable. They are there to help you grow and expand in your consciousness.

Another esoteric truth is that the Universe never gives you more than you can handle. We are made of the same essence as the Universe, which means that everything you need to navigate through life and to flourish in your being, was yours at birth. All you have to do is allow it to flow through you by recognizing it in your self.

Stop telling yourself that you do not have the strength or spirit in you – you are pure strength and spirit incarnated. The 'gift' your problems are 'offering' is the opportunity to remember your own true power. Your 'outer world' is a reflection of your 'inner world'. Therefore, your reality will not change until YOU change.

The solution is not to feel sorry for yourself or to become bitter and withdraw from other people. When you radiate joy, love and trust, you attract people of the same vibrational frequency into your reality. Look in the mirror and recognize yourself as the Creator of your own experiences. You are only as powerless as you tell yourself you are.

188

Pay attention to your thoughts.
YOU believe EVERYTHING
you say to your SELF.
Be kind.

Start telling your self a different story – a story of strength, trust and joy – and watch your life transform.

Thought seeds

189 | *You attract what you think*
and receive what you believe.

When you put an apple seed in the ground you expect an apple tree to grow, right? In fact, you not only expect it, you *know* it will grow. This is so because nature follows the divine law without questioning it: 'what is sowed is received'. As we grow up, we seem to forget that our thoughts are just like the seeds in nature and that our thoughts are 'things' in creation.

190 | *The laws that conduct nature*
are identical to the laws that govern thought.
Every thought is like a seed
that manifests in our reality.
Every single one.

If you had a garden, would you not be careful about the seeds you plant in the soil? Would you not choose beforehand which trees and plants you want to grow in your garden? You would not choose to plant stinging nettles and poison ivy... would you?

Well, we are subconsciously and consciously planting stinging and poisonous thoughts every day in our minds. Instead of planning our 'garden' by visualizing and imagining our desires, wishes and dreams, we let false suggestions from the 'outside world' decide what we are going to occupy our mind with.

191 | *You are ALWAYS giving*
your attention to SOMETHING.
Pay attention to WHAT.
What you focus your mind on, grows.

We let others tell us what to worry about, be afraid of, feel lack from, cry over and stress about. And we allow the wrong seeds to take root and grow, watering them with more fear and worry. Remember that what you focus your mind on, grows. So think about what kind of reality you are habitually cultivating in your 'garden'.

In fact, it is not at all strange that we feel victimized and out of control in our lives, because that is exactly what we ignorantly agree to when we let others plan and design our 'garden'. By choosing to see our reality through the lens of the mass media, politics and corporate economic thinking, we have given up our innate and natural power to decide what kind of experiences we want to fill our lives with. We allow negative sources from the outside to define our inner world.

192 | *We are made in the image*
of a creative God,
which makes us
creative creators.

Since we are constantly creating our own reality, the least we can do is start being observant of what we are creating. Is your garden a creative, inviting, ever-changing field or is it just a habitually repetitive place?

Are you kind to yourself? Can you relax in your garden? Is it a beautiful, luscious oasis? Do you have time to enjoy your garden? How is love expressed there? What kinds of games are being played there?

193 | *You are the master of your thoughts. Be careful what you allow into your mind, because you believe everything you say to yourself.*

You are the one choosing what you think about and project into your reality. You are the one deciding what kind of reality you want to grow in your garden. Is it going to be your fears and worries or your desires and passions?

You are here to explore the beauty of being a creative human being. You are here to explore your desires and joys. You are here to breathe and grow in your garden.

By being consciously aware of your power to choose what you want to create, you can make this garden your own Eden. You are the Gardener, so plant your 'thought seeds' consciously.

194

*Your thoughts are seeds
planted in the soil
of the quantum field.*

*Reality is the garden
you find your self in.*

*When your garden
seems filled with thorns,
look closer...
It might be hiding
beautiful roses...*

Part 11

Why You Are Responsible for Your Reality

Heaven or hell? Your choice

195 | *'Heaven' and 'hell' are states of awareness in the NOW, not 'places' we find ourselves in after we die.*

It is a matter of conscious choice of thoughts, emotions and beliefs, NOW.

Many of us allow 'outer forces' and 'authorities' to mould our perception of ourselves – and to define *who* we are and why we are here – on all levels of existence, including after physical death.

Take, for instance, the doctrinal notions of 'heaven' and 'hell,' which have been used to regulate people's behaviour since the dawn of organized religion. Both these ideas can be used to keep us from exploring our desires and from actually living in the now.

Escaping this reality by living on a promise of a perfect afterlife in heaven or cowering in fear of eternal punishment in hell, are both confining perspectives that can deprive us of full awareness and focus in our experience of our present. Unfortunately, they are also very common ways people use to navigate through physical life.

'Heaven' and 'hell' are not static 'locations' in some afterlife realm where you end up on account of your doings here on Earth. They are states of heart and mind – or more accurately, viewpoints we consciously or unconsciously choose to 'operate' from in our everyday lives.

The way I see it, heaven is created on Earth when you are in alignment with your source: fulfilling your desires and dreams, living your full potential and creating consciously by knowing *what* you want and *who* you are.

Heaven is when you understand that you are a deliberate, conscious creator of your own reality: manifesting for the joy of it, living from a love-based perspective, imagining your life the way YOU want it to be and acting consciously by giving yourself time to think in every situation. In short, experiencing heaven is about consciously creating what YOU desire to explore in your reality.

Hell is the opposite. It is when you are out of alignment with your source: ignoring your dreams and passions, not living your full potential and not knowing what you want or who you are. 'Hell' on Earth is perpetuated by a negative state of mind nurturing limiting beliefs that 'tell' you that you are insignificant and that the reality *'out there'* is dictating the way your life unfolds.

It promotes an existence in which you create your reality from a fear-based perspective – avoiding pain, aimlessly reacting to outer stimuli and often being a victim – instead of creating a life where you are in control and actively seeking joy and abundance. In short, experiencing hell is characterized by the unconscious creation of what you *do not* want in your reality.

And while we are talking about hell and heaven, let's talk about sin. What *is* sin? If you are the embodiment of your desires and you are here to explore who YOU are in time and space, then wouldn't it be fair to call 'hurting' yourself by not following your desires and pursuing your dreams, a sin? Not fulfilling your purpose in life is a violation of the God-given intention of your life. It is to go against the meaning of your existence.

How can I be so sure of all this? Because my childhood was the type of hell I am talking about. And for many years I could not figure out why 'God' would put me in such a place. Until I understood that 'God' was *me* interacting with an unconditionally accepting Universe, giving me the opportunity to use my free will and to explore my creative might.

By offering me polarities to play with and by allowing me to feel how it is to transform thoughts into matter, God showed me how to bend the fabric of the Universe. This gave me the understanding that I chose to be born into 'hell', just so I could experience the immense joy of *creating* 'my own heaven'. Isn't that beautiful?

196

Every experience,
even a negative one,
is valid, accepted and valuable
to All That Is.

You are the imaginer,
creator, explorer and consumer
of all your realities.

Now and for ever.

YOU and your 'demons'

197 | *The only way to 'see' clearly*
and act consciously
is through the frequency of love.

Love gives energy.
Hate requires energy.

Anger is a 'demon' that feeds off your *energy* – if you allow it to roam, plunder and feast off your body and mind.

Resentment is a 'demon' that feeds off your *soul* – if you allow it to fester and 'guide' you.

Victimhood is a 'demon' that feeds off your *spirit* – if you allow its bittersweet 'embrace' to hold you tight.

Envy and Jealousy are 'demons' that feed off your *life force* – if you allow their poisonous grip around your heart.

Guilt is a 'demon' that feeds off your *spiritual identity* – if you allow it to sit on your chest and chew on your self-worth.

I have chosen to call these emotional states 'demons' because, just like in the medieval descriptions of the doings of demons, they 'take possession' of your being while distorting your perception of reality by tampering with your judgement.

It might feel almost impossible not to react to them and even harder to get rid of them once you have allowed them into your system, because they 'create' smokescreens, illusions and misunderstandings to keep you in the game – until you are drained of physical and emotional energy.

The only way to 'see' clearly and act consciously is to take responsibility for your own state of mind – by actively 'banning' these low-frequency feelings out of your system. Changing your frequency *on demand* – by deliberately choosing not to react to the outer trigger while focusing your awareness and attention on feelings of gratitude, appreciation and love – is not an easy task. Yet it is the only way to regain your true self and to realign with your source.

Understanding that YOU are the master of your inner world – and by this, also the master of the outer expression and manifestation of it – is what expanding in your consciousness ultimately means. It is also what the ancient spiritual practice of inner illumination (allowing the light from within to illuminate your being) actually is all about.

198 | *Every time you choose*
LOVE over hate,
LOVE over fear,
LOVE over anger,
you change your frequency
from scarcity to abundance.

Stay in LOVE.

Knowing who you truly are and being aligned to your source creates a *high-frequency* 'space' that does not allow *low-*

frequency 'demons' to enter your being. Because standing in the frequency of love means to *under-stand* your Higher Self – to literally stand under the 'protection' and in the 'space' of your unconditionally loving source.

Wayne Dyer eloquently states, 'How people treat you is their karma; how you react is yours.' What this means is that we are *all* responsible for our *own* frequency.

199 | *You cannot do anything*
to change another person's action,
but you can change
your reaction to it.

Your inner world is
YOUR domain.

With every argument, misunderstanding or disagreement, ask yourself:

200 | *What am I adding to the situation?*
Love or guilt?
Calmness or anger?
Clarity or confusion?

You are always the source to your feelings. No matter what the conditions are. Take anger, for instance: sometimes anger is necessary, but natural anger only lasts for around 15 seconds. Prolonged anger is a choice. And so is every other negative feeling. A choice. *Your choice.*

So, truth be told, no one else can make you unhappy or angry. You are the one allowing the feelings by choosing to react to someone else's beliefs. You are responsible for which 'demons' you invite and allow into the interaction and exchange of energies.

Ultimately:

201

You are responsible for everything you think, say and do in your life.

You are responsible for your life.
No one else but you.

Your world and the 'real world'

202 | *We are the dreamers,*
dreaming a dream of life...

Some dreams are bad.
Some dreams are good.

Hold on to the good ones...

Since I truly believe that every soul has its origin in an unconditionally loving source and as a consequence of that, all beings are essentially good, I have always tried to focus my awareness on the brightest side of every encounter in my reality.

My positive views on being human and about the fabric of reality have, however, often put me in fruitless arguments with people who see reality through a negative lens. Countless are the occasions where I have found myself defending my affirmative thoughts on reality and being treated as if I were kidding myself, or living in some self-deceiving dream.

Usually I get comments such as 'It is not that easy in the real world' or 'Try living in the real world and you might change your mind.' Both these statements beg the question, *What does the 'real world' actually mean?*

Don't we all live in the real world? Is there an 'outside world' that is more real than the world I perceive? Why would that world be more real than the world I perceive? If by 'the real world' those people mean the quantum field of possibilities (All That Is, the Universe, Source, God), then yes, it is more real because it contains everything, allows everything and is everything, now and for ever. It is simply All That Is.

But if they are referring to this physical illusion we are exploring through our bodies and five senses in time and space, then the 'real world' is very much dependent on each subjective mind imagining, manifesting and consuming it.

I think the American writer and poet Edgar Allan Poe came very close to describing the truth about what physical reality actually is with these words: 'All that we see or seem... Is but a dream within a dream.'

The real question, then, is not about establishing the 'realness' of the 'outside' world but about why so many of us are choosing to perceive a nightmare dictated by others when we could choose to imagine a more lucid dream of beauty, abundance and love into existence.

Because, make no mistake:

203 | *Physical life is a dream, and we are the dreamers choosing what we want to explore and experience.*

The more awake we are, the more this dream of physical reality becomes lucid; and the more we can influence, change and transform it. Think about this: if the world 'outside' you is a reflection of the world 'inside' you, then how can the reflection be more real than the ONE looking at it?

It will reflect an objective mirror image – based on the information sent to it – without altering it. The information it is reflecting comes from the one looking into the mirror. It is an objective image of YOU – your preferences, desires, wants, needs, fears, don't wants... It is all there, staring back at you as a 'solid' reality, objectively reflecting everything YOU subjectively are.

204 | *Reality is what YOU*
think,
imagine,
believe,
dream,
fear or
hope it to be.

I have come to realize that people with a positive perspective on life and those with a negative one have difficulty understanding each other because they are not speaking the same 'language'. The words and sentences sound the same, but they carry different energetic blueprints that originate from different 'places' in the body.

205 | *The difference between*
a negative and a positive
view on reality is:

One comes from your MIND,
the other from your HEART.

Let me explain: a positive interpretation of reality seems to come from the *heart*, with an emotional flavour attached to it, while a negative interpretation seems to come from the *mind* and has an intellectual flavour.

Intellect is connected to time and space because it requires linear, cause-and-effect thinking, while emotion is more instant and intuitive and is thus less dependent on time and space.

206 | *In a battle between a feeling (heart) and a thought (mind), feeling ALWAYS wins.*

This is why comedy, poetry, art, music, dance, play, laughter, love and passion allow us to grasp bigger glimpses of the truth about our reality. The fabric your reality is made of is infinite and eternal. Since your source is unconditionally accepting and all-encompassing and you are expressing and manifesting that essence into the world, the truth about it cannot be fully described by your mind. It can only be felt emotionally, through your heart.

There is a scene in the 1997 science-fiction movie *Contact* that beautifully illustrates this. A young scientist called Ellie Arroway is sent through a wormhole to visit a star in the constellation Vega. During her journey through time and space she sees a celestial light show up close.

The event touches her deeply and even though she is used to processing information intellectually, she loses her ability to describe in words what she is witnessing. All she can manage to articulate is: '*No... no words. No words to describe it... Poetry! They should have sent a poet. So beautiful... So beautiful... I had no idea.*'

207 | *You feel...*
... that which is real.

Worker or Creator? Your choice

208 | *Stop doing things that are not in alignment with who you are.*

If it does not evolve you or make you happy, be courageous and walk away!

There is a persistent and pervasive belief in the Western world that we must spend every second of our lives being 'productive'. This way of thinking is instilled in us at an early age and is later on perpetuated by the culture we grow up in and the society in which we live.

This mindset requires human creativity to be squeezed into perfect time slots in which we are supposed to adapt our imagination and compress our creativity into the bits of time 'given' to us. Five days a week, from nine to five. Year in and year out.

Time is compartmentalized into neat 'boxes' labelled 'work', 'private life', 'weekday' and 'holiday'. This fragmentation of time denies you a complete view of your self and of your place in reality. And since it requires you to change your personality back and forth, just to fit in or function, it allows you no holistic view of who YOU are, either.

You have a 'work self' and a 'home self'. Your children or partner would not recognize you if you continued to be your 'work self' when you came home and your co-workers would eat you alive if you came to work being your 'home self'. Jumping back and forth in this manner deprives you of vital energy. Bit by bit, this kind of lifestyle 'steals' your true identity.

209 | *You are a free spirit put here by your soul's desire to explore who YOU are and what you LOVE to do.*

What kind of reality does not encourage *all* its sentient beings to explore the purpose of their existence? Ask yourself why there are no 'boxes' labelled 'total freedom' and 'me'. Or even better, ask yourself why we need these 'boxes' altogether. Our entire society is built around people *working*, not on doing what they *love*. But, when you understand that YOU create your own reality – and I mean *literally* create it – you also know the answer to why there is so little true freedom in our society.

Let me clarify what I mean by 'true freedom'. The way I see it, true freedom is closely connected to the concept of abundance, which is a birthright.

210 | *Abundance is a birthright.*
It equals freedom, as in:

Physical freedom.
Spiritual freedom.
Intellectual freedom.
Financial freedom.

Most of us accept the reality we live in, as it is, because 'it has always been so'. Subconsciously, we have been co-creating a reality, without questioning it, based on limiting beliefs that have held most of us in constant *'sleep-state low-frequency-servant-mode'* since the dawn of civilization.

We need to wake up from our mental slumber and understand that the only way to change our reality is to shift our perspective from perceiving ourselves as 'workers', to knowing that we are deliberate creators of our own opportunities. It does not matter what you are 'supposed' to do or what your culture or society 'wants' you to do. It does not matter what the outer circumstances are.

211 | *The only thing*
that really matters
is what YOU want to do.
Because this is YOUR reality
and YOU are in charge of
everything in it.

You can start by making a list of the things that you love doing. Ask yourself: 'If money was not an issue, what would I be doing?' No matter how 'impossible' your dreams might seem to others or to yourself, just play with your thoughts and imagine how you would feel, doing what you love.

When you eliminate the emotional and mental 'block' that a lack of money usually puts between you and your desires – and in doing so raise your frequency – you open your mind to opportunities in your reality that are invisible to you when you are in a state of low energy.

To heighten your frequency you need to think about the things that make you feel happy, proud, grateful, prosperous and abundant. Every thing created in this world started off as a thought in someone's mind.

212 | *When you start imagining how YOU want your life to unfold, you invite the possibilities into YOUR reality and life.*

Time is the only 'currency' we have. Imagine time as a limited amount of 'money' in your wallet. You are paying for every thing you experience in your life. Would you willingly pay for ALL the experiences you currently have in your life? Because, know the truth: that is what you are doing. Start choosing consciously what you want to spend your 'time-currency' on.

Your 'Buddha-In-Disguise'

213 | *You will keep attracting*
'bad' situations
into your reality until:

1. You see the pattern.
2. GET THE MESSAGE.
3. Make a change.

We all have recurring problems, situations and obstacles in our lives. How you choose to handle a negatively charged situation can tell you a great deal about yourself and show you new aspects of who you truly are.

In that sense:

214 | *All obstacles are actually 'portals'*
through which you can expand
in your consciousness – by learning
new things about who you are.

If you keep avoiding the problem and ignoring the pattern it is creating in your life, it will reappear over and over again with increasing impact, until you deal with it. We live in an expanding Universe that wants you to *push* your boundaries so it can *grow through* you.

215 | *You are not here to suffer.*
You are here to learn
new things about your self
and expand in your consciousness.

If you have the courage to ask yourself *why* you are responding and reacting in the way you are when encountering an obstacle or a recurring problem – and be open-minded enough to act on the answers with integrity and *full responsibility* – you have an opportunity to actually 'change your stars'.

The trick is to look at the problem *without 'outsourcing' the cause.* It is so easy to blame others for our unhappiness, anger, stress and emotional pain. But by 'outsourcing' the root of our discomfort we not only give away our power to resolve it, we also lose the benefit of learning the lesson we need in order to grow.

216 | *You cannot change*
what you do not own.

Own your problem
by recognizing your
part in it.

Since your vibratory state (frequency) determines what you attract and experience in your immediate reality, an important question to ask yourself is: 'What in my frequency do I need to change in order to get a different manifestation?'

Unless you are a child, *you* are the one responsible for your own wellbeing and happiness. By recognizing the problem pattern and acting on it honestly, you can transform the limitations and inertia that are a result of the unsolved problem into freedom and enjoyment in the present.

Because, as we all know:

217 | *It is in the conflicts,*
problems and obstacles
that the greatest possibilities
for growth and illumination reside.

This is actually one of the main reasons why the negative aspect of our reality exists. The Universe is not serving you negatively charged situations because it is working against you. You were not born under an unlucky star.

A recurring problem or obstacle is a reminder that you have unresolved issues affecting your frequency in a negative way. It is your soul telling you that you are out of alignment with your source and that you are not in tune with your natural frequency. This deviation from the frequency of your source and who you truly are, expresses itself as emotional or physical pain and results in suffering.

In that sense:

218 | *An obstacle is just a reminder*
to adjust your frequency,
and to align with your source.
Nothing more. Nothing less.

Your source emanates the high frequency of unconditional love, joy and abundance, which means that the low frequency of suffering cannot 'get' you there. Actually, suffering will never 'get' you anywhere – at least not where you consciously want to be.

Suffering serves a purpose only as a wake-up call, but the suffering as such should be limited. Suffering is a 'tool' you can use to learn something new about yourself. Though in the long run, it is not a beneficial frequency to stay in.

To heighten your frequency away from suffering, you need to acknowledge the real problem without dwelling on it. You need to ask yourself how you attracted it, without allowing the information to trap you into guilt and remorse. Remember: there are no mistakes, only feedback. When you have figured out the subconscious belief behind the frequency that attracted the problem, you have learned your 'lesson', received your 'message' or gained your 'wisdom', and you can let it go.

I know that this can sometimes be hard to do. But if you can tilt your perspective a bit and see the obstacle as a little 'Buddha-in-Disguise' giving you great opportunities to evolve, you will be able to come closer to your soul-source and allow yourself to change your future in a constructive and beneficial way, while at the same time, letting go of emotional 'baggage' such as suffering, regret and guilt.

The message your problems and obstacles are giving you is not, dwell on your suffering, be a victim, feel sorry for yourself, give up... What your little 'Buddha-in-Disguise' is trying to communicate to you is: everything is solvable; everything is a learning opportunity. Enjoy the joy of unveiling *more of who you are*.

219

*Obstacles always
present opportunities.*

*Valuable information
about yourself is imbedded
in your reaction to a problem.*

*Use the feedback to
change your path,
rethink your strategies
and above all, to SEEK JOY!*

The Wisdom Keeper

220 | *You are the keeper*
of the wisdom you seek.

Look within.
Allow it to speak.

I am grateful for the loneliness – and even appreciate the alienation – I felt as a child because it focused my awareness inwards and allowed me to explore the inner silence where my true self hides.

This inner exploration revealed to me that there is so much more to reality and life than just survival. We are not here to struggle our way through existence and then, when the time comes, simply lie down and die. To me, even at an early age, physical reality seemed to be about exploring new things and about enjoying the pure fact of being alive – no matter how hard life sometimes presented itself to be.

Being fully in the NOW-moment by breathing in and out felt like much more than just breathing to survive. Observing a butterfly dance through the air or enjoying the rain on my face was enough of an experience to justify the reason for my existence – actually, the reason for *all* of existence.

Most of us are so preoccupied with the constant chatter created in our minds by fear and abstract problems – keeping us in habitual 'survival mode' – that we fail to see the magic and beauty in the most ordinary and simple things as a butterfly or a raindrop.

Paradoxically, in order to silence the noise in our heads, we tend to search for more information from the *outside*, as if acquiring it will miraculously ease our restless minds and give us time, somewhere in the *future*, to enjoy the inner peace we so ache for *now*.

What seems to elude us is that, in order to reach our goal of calmness and happiness 'somewhere in the future', we must stop chasing information 'outside' of our selves and start embracing what we already know from within *now*. And to allow the inner wisdom stored in our soul to reveal itself through our selves by interacting mindfully and consciously with our reality now.

221

Quieten down.
Breathe in and out
for the simple joy
of breathing.

Create time in your mind to think
and space in your heart to be.

Some years ago, I saw an interesting documentary about the pyramids in Egypt called *The Pyramid Code*, directed by Carmen Boulter PhD. One of the people being interviewed was an elderly man called Abd'el Hakim Awyan. The always smiling Hakim could best be described as a 'walking library', with a mind filled with long-forgotten ancient memories and knowledge of sacred universal truths and principles. The interesting thing about Hakim was not only that he was a very knowledgeable man, but he also defined himself as a *container* of that valuable information.

He called himself a wisdom keeper. His total awareness of the inner riches he had gathered during a happy and fulfilling life, and his definition of himself as a guardian of this treasure, resonated perfectly with me. Listening to him, I realized that in a sense, we are all wisdom keepers – storing the accumulated knowledge of our lives in our minds and hearts. All we have to do is start connecting to that knowledge and embracing the wisdom we have within.

I decided to call myself a wisdom keeper because I, like the smiling Hakim, collect my experiences and explorations in the physical world and extract the wisdom imbedded in every thing I encounter, regardless of whether it is an obstacle or pure joy. I honour everything that has happened in my life and use the knowledge and wisdom I have gathered to elevate my own consciousness. And by sharing my knowledge with others, who allow my thoughts into their reality, I thereby also help raise our collective consciousness.

222

You are the keeper of your inner wisdom.

Dive into it.
Explore it.
Enjoy it.
Share it.

The creative side of responsibility

Most of us do not like the word 'responsibility' because we tend to connect it with feelings of inadequacy, guilt and victimhood. But, being responsible is simply about being the one able to respond in a certain situation. Taking responsibility for something is the same as taking ownership of it.

You cannot change what you do not own, so taking responsibility for your thoughts, feelings and actions, is to take ownership of yourself and your part of creation. Viewed from this perspective, responsibility has nothing to do with guilt and inadequacy and everything to do with creativity and freedom.

My thoughts and this book are a part of my belief system. I cannot prove the things I 'play' with in my heart and mind, but every sentence I write is *my* truth. It will feel true for those operating on the same frequency as me and false to those of a different frequency. In the end, it is all about what truth we *choose* to see and believe in.

To me, one easy way to take responsibility for what we allow into this world is to always:

223 | *Speak your TRUTH through LOVE, or say nothing at all.*

As you now know, on a quantum level of reality, thoughts behave like things. The more you believe in a thought, the more 'solid' it becomes, and the more it affects the infinite field around you. It does not matter if the thought is positive or negative or whether you want it or not.

A belief is a cluster of repetitive thoughts that you believe in. The more thoughts of the same vibration, the stronger the belief and the more likely it is for that thought to manifest. Now, multiply this with all the people on Earth and you have a 'solid' reality perpetually manifesting itself. This is the simple reason why you and each and every one of us must take full responsibility for what we think and believe into being.

I strongly believe that ignorance is the negative root of all injustice, pain, greed, fear and war. The opposite of ignorance is knowledge. Consider this:

224 | *If you do not know who you truly are, then every action is an unconscious action.*

So, figuring out who YOU are will make your actions more conscious. And an action coming from consciousness cannot be based in ignorance. The more conscious you are of *who* you are, the more understanding, compassion and love you will emanate, because that is what the essence of consciousness *is* – unconditional love of All That Is. It is the unconscious ones who are capable of manifesting ignorance, creating greed, poverty and scarcity. It is a question of realizing your true self – not your conditioned self.

When my son was in second grade I tried to teach him how to defend himself when other boys would pick on him in the schoolyard. I went down on my knees and asked him to push me as hard as he could. But he just stood there, doing nothing. So I asked him, 'Why don't you push me?' He looked at me with sadness in his eyes and replied, 'But if I push them, they will be hurt, won't they?'

This got me at my core because I realized that I had allowed my conditioned self to override my inherent wisdom about how the Universe actually works. The question my son evoked in me was: 'How can retaliation ever be an option? In what way would it solve the problem by adding more victims to it?' This is deep wisdom coming from an eight-year-old boy. What he was teaching me was in fact an esoteric truth:

225

Everything you see, sees you.
Everything you hear, talks to you.
Everything you touch, touches you back.

This is the true meaning of Oneness. Being conscious is understanding that you cannot change others – everyone has his or her own path to walk. Knowing this, violence and force become irrelevant. You understand your place in this reality as one with everything that surrounds you. This means that if you act arrogantly, violently or maliciously towards others, you will automatically hurt yourself by the vibration you emanate and by literally standing in the frequency of hate and fear.

I realized that my son had a more expanded version of consciousness than I did. If I was going to keep up, I needed to open up, listen more and allow myself to expand. Since then I follow a rule – every choice I make must pass my 'love filter'. In everything I encounter that requires me to make a choice, I ask myself, 'Is there love in this?' If the answer is 'no', *I do not allow it to pass through me into my reality and into this world.* Instead, I take the time to look for alternatives with more love in them.

226

Be conscious of what YOU are allowing THROUGH you into this reality.

Be the place where LOVE manifests in time and space.

It is your responsibility to unveil your demons of fear, worry and negative feelings and see them for what they are. It is your responsibility to actively seek out what gives you calmness, peace, joy and happiness. It is your responsibility to say 'no' to sadness, misery and victimhood. Everything in your reality is neutral in itself. It is your interpretation – and above all, your *reaction* to it – that charges it with a specific frequency matching your perception, beliefs and interpretation.

Your thoughts are energetic vibrational 'places' that you 'visit' and dwell in. That is why you need to choose the mood of your thoughts wisely.

227 | *Your mind is your internal 'vision board'.*
| *Do not fill it with things you fear or want to avoid.*
| *Focus on what you desire and want.*

Create the atmosphere you enjoy. These are YOUR thoughts, YOUR interpretations, YOUR emotions and YOUR beliefs. Do whatever you want with them. YOU are the source. You are in control. Realizing that you are the creator of your own reality and co- creator of our collective reality puts you in a powerful position.

The more you know the immense range of your own power, the more your imagination becomes a tool of creation. And the more visualizing and daydreaming become an integral and important part of your everyday life.

228 | *Taking responsibility for everything in your reality sets you FREE.*
| *CHANGE what you can. Keep what you LOVE. FORGIVE the rest.*

Exploring who YOU are is to be responsible for what you create. You do not need to take time to understand who you truly are. Your true self and source is with you all the time. Everything in your reality is a reflection of YOU. Everything around you contains answers to who you truly are. Every single thing you choose to focus your awareness on is synchronistically connected to you and thus contains a 'message' about your relationship to it.

The answer to who you are is imbedded in the connection between '*in here*' and '*out there*', and in how YOU choose to explore it. Getting to know yourself is like a beautiful dance between you and the Universe. You can never finish it because knowing who you are is not a destination to reach but a dance to dance or a game to play for the joy of experiencing who YOU are now and what you want to become in the future.

229 | *Exploring who you are in the physical world is an ongoing process of becoming more aware of the SOURCE to who YOU are.*

Life is like an ocean. Sometimes it is calm, pleasant and enjoyable and sometimes it is pushing, demanding, fighting. So, even when you worry and feel stressed, know that it will pass and life will become beautiful and peaceful again soon. Because you see, balance is a constant law of the Universe. And so is change. The two are always interacting, always creating motion. YOU are the stillness in between.

230 | *The art of being*
'the captain of your soul'
is to:

TRUST your SELF
when life is hard.

ENJOY yourself
when life is GOOD.

If today was my last day and I got to tell you only three truths about life, these are the ones I would leave you with:

1. You create your own reality and everything in it: *literally*. There is no power outside of you. PLAY more.

2. You are eternal. There is nothing to fear. EXPLORE more.

3. Love is All That Is. ENJOY more.

I would also share the secret of your true identity with you:

231 | *Put your hand on your heart*
and repeat after me:

I am the light in the darkness.
I am the love in the hate.
I am the calmness in the storm.
I am the courage in the fear.

ABOUT THE AUTHOR

Hubert M. Biernat

Gordana Biernat is a thinker, writer, speaker and wisdom keeper. She is one of Oprah Winfrey's SuperSoul 100 teachers – a collection of 100 awakened leaders who are using their voices and talent to elevate humanity.

Gordana holds Master of Arts in Art History. She has also studied Psychology, Communication and Media.

As a speaker, Gordana talks about the perception of reality, consciousness, creativity, leadership and art. As a writer, she influences conscious communications through higher thought. She has been featured on Oprah.com, and has written for many major news aggregators and blogs, as well as print magazines and publications, including *The Huffington Post* and *The Times of India*.

As a thinker, Gordana shares her thoughts on Twitter, initiating creative processes and conscious communication. She is a mentor, assisting those who seek self-development and a greater sense of being through intellectual and spiritual inquiry.

When not on assignment, Gordana enjoys life, her family, serious reading and food and wine.

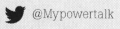 @Mypowertalk    GordanaBiernat

 info@mypowertalk.com

www.mypowertalk.com